VISUAL GUIDE :: CASA MILÀ

La Pedrera

PHOTOGRAPHS: CARLOS GIORDANO AND NICOLÁS PALMISANO

D0971489

GUÍAS VISUALES
GRANDES OBRAS

01

contents

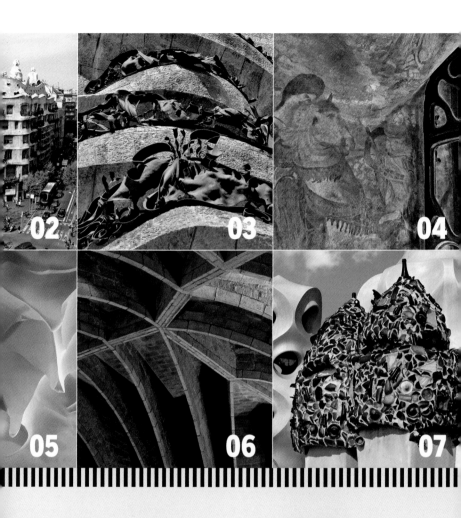

01

The origins of La Pedrera

Barcelona grows as industry and trade develops

At unstoppable pace towards an industrialized and modern society, Barcelona grows and is transformed. In the year 1888, it hosts the first Universal Exhibition of Spain, succeeding in ranking the city amongst the most important in Europe. It is a period of intense cultural life and recuperation of Catalan values. Within this context, a few years later, will appear Antoni Gaudí's stroke of genius: La Pedrera.

The spirit of the period

In the last third of the 19th century Catalonia underwent a great cultural renewal, reflected, above all, in literature, music, plastic arts and architecture. This movement, called the *Renaixença* (Renaissance), promoted Catalan, which had been confined to the privacy of the home, as a cultural language. The revival of Catalan values, along with the growth of Barcelona's industry and commerce, resulted in the formation of nationalist political tendencies that spread throughout all fields.

Barcelona in 1880
Towards the end of the 19th century, the city of Barcelona had already developed into a great metropolis.

1892
IS THE YEAR
in which the *Unió Catalanista* draws up the draft of the *Constitución Regional Catalana*, which calls for an autonomous government for Catalonia.

Industry
With the growth of the Industrial Revolution a great quantity of factories transform Catalonia into provider of Spain.

 CHRONOLOGY
KEY FACTS ABOUT GAUDÍ'S PERIOD

1853
Otis invents the lift
Elisha G. Otis presents the first life with anti-fall device.

1863
The London tube is inaugurated. It was the first underground railway in the world.

1867
First volume of *The Capital*
In this essay Karl Marx drew up a dissection of the capitalist system.

1870
Third French Republic. The King Louis Napoleon III abdicated after the defeat of France in the war against Prussia.

The Victory Arch
Constructed by architect Josep Vilaseca in the year 1888, the arch acted as main entrance to the Universal Exhibition of Barcelona.

The Universal Exhibition

In the year 1888, Barcelona hosted the first Universal Exhibition of Spain; aiming to promote the country as an industrial power and so extend its foreign trade. The city council therefore projected numerous urban developments that would transform Barcelona into a great European city.

1888

IS WHEN
Ciutadella Park is inaugurated, home to the first Universal Exhibition of Barcelona. More than 1,000 men worked non-stop on its construction.

The splendour of the industrial bourgeoisie

Catalonia, with the city of Barcelona at its helm, was the Spanish region that most quickly absorbed the changes provoked by the Industrial Revolution. While the rest of Spain continued being basically agricultural, in Catalonia a sound industrial framework was being created. This economic prosperity led to the rise of a flourishing industrial bourgeoisie that would become promoter, whether as client or patron, of numerous artistic and architectonic projects.

 DATA
TEXTILE INDUSTRY IN CATALONIA

The textile industry was pioneering in its use of steam machinery.

Textile mills:	Manual	Mechanical
1841	24.880	231
1850	24.008	5.580
1861	12.026	9.695

1874
Cézanne sells his first painting, *Maison du Pendu.* The artist was ignored in his time.

1876
Alfonso XII King of Spain. Exiled from the age of 11, he recovered the throne for the Bourbons.

1879
Edison invented the electric bulb
This invention generalizes electrical illumination.

Passeig de Gràcia and La Pedrera

The most important avenue in Barcelona is created

Barcelona grows in population and expanse. The approval of the urban development plan for the Eixample, links the old nucleus of the city with the municipalities on the outskirts. Passeig de Gràcia is created and is rapidly transformed into the main artery of the city and is chosen by the bourgeoisie to construct stunning architectonic projects. It is there that Antoni Gaudí plans Casa Milà, popularly known as La Pedrera.

The Eixample

At the beginning of the 19th century Barcelona experienced an unprecedented demographic explosion. Growing industry attracted thousands of workers and the city, surrounded by an ancient wall, could no longer hold all its inhabitants. The sanitary situation was very poor and the cholera epidemic of 1854 hastened the decision to knock down the walls. The demolishment made way for the Eixample, an urban project devised by the engineer Cerdà and approved in 1859. It consisted of a great network of perpendicular and parallel streets in which the blocks had chamfered corners or bevelled edges that facilitated visibility, with construction only permitted on two sides and the remainder dedicated to gardens.

The Eixample. Barcelona's urban expansion project was planned in a way that every zone would have all services: schools, hospitals, markets etc.

Ildefons Cerdà, the creator of the Eixample
The town planner devised a city to be enjoyed by all of its inhabitants.

CHRONOLOGY
KEY FACTS ABOUT GAUDÍ'S PERIOD

1883
The Chicago School. After the city fire in 1871, various skyscrapers were built.

1887
The automobile is born. Benz and Daimler boosted the automobile industry with the combustion motor.

1889
The Eiffel Tower is inaugurated
It was constructed for the Universal Exhibition of Paris of 1889.

The fashionable avenue
At the beginning of the 20th century, Passeig de Gràcia was the most prestigious artery of the city. Barcelonans would go out and stroll along the stretch of avenue, perusing the windows of its luxury shops or going to the theatre.

La Pedrera
In a popular Passeig de Gràcia and in the year 1910, La Pedrera, still unfinished, had only one of its balconies exhibiting railings. Antoni Gaudí signed the end of the construction work in the year 1912, after more than six years of work since its commission by Pere Milà in 1905.

Passeig de Gràcia

The city's most important thoroughfare was, in the past, the shortest route between the city of Barcelona and the town of Gràcia, a small locality situated three kilometres away. On either side of the avenue, the fountains, gardens and recreational areas drew the Barcelonans. With the city's expansion, the avenue became the Eixample's spinal cord. In 1905, now illuminated and paved, the main means of transport begin to circulate and the avenue is chosen by the wealthiest of personalities for the construction of their homes, designed by prestigious architects. The Milà family decide, within this context, to entrust their house to an ingenious architect: Antoni Gaudí.

1908
ALFONSO XII'S VISIT. The *Juventud Monárquica* (Youth Royalists) received the king in the city's most important avenue, Passeig de Gràcia.

Passeig de Gràcia today. At present, the avenue still maintains its elegance and architectonic splendour intact.

1894
Invention of the radio. The Italian Marconi was the first who managed to transmit radio signals.

1895
First cinema projection
It took place in Paris, organized by the Lumière brothers.

1898
Independence of Cuba. The war of Spain against the United States led to the loss of Cuba.

1899
Foundation of F.C. Barcelona
A Swiss residing in Barcelona, Johan Camper, was its founder.

The promoters, the Milà family

They commission a house and Gaudí projects a work of art

A married couple, the Milàs, wanted to live in Barcelona's new Eixample, a fashionable area of great prestige. Subsequently, they bought a large sized plot of land on the corner of Passeig de Gràcia and Provença Street, the former municipal boundary between the city of Barcelona and the town of Gràcia. To carry out the project, Pere Milà contracted one of the most innovative architects of the time, Antoni Gaudí.

The Milà family

Pere Milà i Camps was a businessman who came from a distinguished Catalan family; his father was a textile industrialist and his uncle Josep had been Mayor of Barcelona in 1899. Roser Segimon i Artells, originally from Reus, got married at the age of 22 to Josep Guardiola i Grau, a Spaniard who had made his fortune in Latin America, 38 years older than her, and on his death in 1901 she inherited all his fortune. Pere and Roser met each other in the French spa of Vichy, they married in 1903 and in 1905 they entrusted Gaudí with the design of their house: La Pedrera.

Roser Segimon
She inherited her fortune from her first husband, Josep Guardiola.

Pere Milà
Elegant and with a busy social life, he dedicated himself to politics for many years, becoming Member of Parliament for the *Solidaritat Catalana*.

1905
IS THE YEAR
In which the Milàs bought the plot measuring 34 by 56 metres on which La Pedrera would be built.

The *Monumental*. Pere Milà was the owner of this bullring.

CHRONOLOGY
KEY FACTS ABOUT GAUDÍ'S PERIOD

1900
Zeppelin flight
The German Count Ferdinand von Zeppelin invented this aircraft lighter than air.

1900
Freud publishes *The Interpretation of Dreams*. The Austrian doctor sets out the basis for the theory of psychoanalysis.

1903
First piloted flight
The brothers Wilbur and Orville Wright invented the first aeroplane with engine.

The block of discord. In the same block on Passeig de Gràcia, Puig i Cadafalch built Casa Amatller. Doménech i Montaner built Casa Lleó Morera and Gaudí finished the renovation of the Casa Batlló.

Gaudí and Modernism

Between the end of the 19th century and the start of the 20th century, Modernism transforms the city of Barcelona. The rupture with the past, the search for a new style and the desire for modernity stretched across the arts. At its maximum expression, architecture knew how to integrate traditional trades such as ceramic work, wrought iron, stained glass windows and sculpture, creating magnificent works of art below an ideal of modernist beauty. Within this context, Antoni Gaudí stood out amongst the architects of the period, generating a style and a work that was more expressive and personal.

Palau de la Música
Constructed between 1905 and 1908 by the architect Lluís Domènech i Montaner, the palace was decorated by sculptors Eusebi Arnau and Pau Gargallo.

Casaramona factory
For this work, Puig i Cadafalch obtained the award from the City Council for best building of 1912.

Domènech i Montaner
He was one of the most important and well-known architects of Modernism.

Puig i Cadafalch
His work combines Gothic-Catalan elements with Nordic influence.

1905
Einstein announces the theory of relativity. The German scientist revolutionized the classical concepts of physics.

1908
Auguste Rodin sculpts *The Kiss*
This work is, together with *The Thinker*, the sculptor's most famous work.

1911
Amudsen arrives at the South Pole
The Norwegian explorer was the first to reach the South Pole.

1912
The *Titanic* sinks
On the night of the 14th of April, on its maiden voyage, the great ocean liner goes down.

Gaudí, the architect in fashion

With total freedom, Gaudí plans his last civil work

Captivated by Casa Batlló, Pere Milà entrusts Antoni Gaudí with the construction of his home. It was 1905 and the 54-year-old architect was in his professional prime. Mature personally as well as artistically, Gaudí would carry out a daring, complex and expensive project, which encountered problems with the City Council as well as the actual Milà family, but was transformed into a masterpiece: La Pedrera.

The commission

Pere Milà was left awestruck after seeing the house Gaudí had renovated for Josep Batlló, his father's business partner, and this was how he decided to entrust the project of his new house to this prestigious architect. The Milà family wanted to construct a large building within which they would occupy the main floor (*el principal*) and the rest would be given over to rented apartments, which was very common amongst the bourgeoisie of the time. In September 1905, Pere Milà applied for the permits to demolish the former chalet of three storeys situated on the plot he had bought on Passeig de Gràcia, and on the 2nd of February of the following year, the actual architect put forward the plans and asked the City Council for building permission.

Antoni Gaudí
When the architect started work on La Pedrera, he was working on six other projects: Casa Batlló, Sagrada Familia, Park Güell, the Güell Colony Church, Torre Bellesguard and the restoration of the Cathedral of Palma de Mallorca.

CHRONOLOGY
KEY FACTS ABOUT GAUDÍ'S PERIOD

1914
The First World War
Known as the Great War, it involved 32 countries.

1916
Birth of Dadaism
This artistic movement surged as a criticism of western culture.

DADA
DADA
DADA
was ist DADA?
☞ Philosophie?
Religion?

1917
The Russian Revolution
After overthrowing the Tsar, Russia became a Soviet state.

The study of Sagrada Familia. It was there that Gaudí drew the first sketches for La Pedrera project.

A complicated relationship

Throughout construction numerous differences surged between Gaudí and the Milà family. One of the problems was that the architect went well over budget on various occasions as well as using more than the permitted building space, which then led to problems with the City Council. The disputes were aggravated by a matter of fees, which was brought to the attention of the Barcelona Tribunal Court, which ruled in favour of the architect in 1915.

54
YEARS OLD
was Gaudí's age when he took on the commission of La Pedrera.

Gaudí's last civil work
La Pedrera was the fourth work on Passeig de Gràcia. Prior to it were the Gilbert pharmacy (1879), the Bar Torino (1902) and Casa Batlló (1906).

The life of Antoni Gaudí

1852
He is born on the 25th of June in Reus.

1868
He moves to Barcelona to study architecture.

1875
He does military service.

1876
He collaborates with the architect Del Villar on the Ciutadella Park. • His brother and mother die.

1878
He finished his architecture studies. • Designs the lampposts for the Plaça Reial and Pla del Palau. • Projects the Workers' Cooperative of Mataro. • Exhibits in the Universal Exhibition of Paris of 1878.

1883
The Caprice is started, in Comillas, and is finished in 1885. • He starts work on Casa Vincens, which he finishes in 1888. • He takes control of the work on Sagrada Familia.

1889
He constructs the Episcopal Palace of Astorga and the Casa de los Botines.

1900
Casa Calvet is awarded prize for best building. Park Güell is started.

1904
He is commissioned to renovate the Casa Batlló.

1906
La Pedrera is commenced. He moves to Park Güell with his father and niece. Some months after, his father dies at the age of 93.

1910
Receives the commission for a hotel in New York.

1911
Ill with Maltese fever he moves to Puigcerdà, where he draws up his will.

1912
His niece Rosita dies.

1914
Work is interrupted on Park Güell.

1918
His friend and patron, Eusebi Güell, dies.

1925
He moves into his study in Sagrada Familia.

1926
On the 7th of June he is knocked down by a tram. Three days later he dies at the age of 74.

Plaça Reial lamppost

1918
The Great War ends. German surrender put an end to the war. Around 10 million people died.

1919
Gropius founds the Bauhaus
This German school was one of the most influential in modern art.

1923
Dictatorship of Primo de Rivera
This military man headed the *coup d'état* and led Spain until 1930.

1926
Television is invented
The Scot John Logie Baird was the first to transmit moving images.

GAUDÍ'S MOST IMPORTANT WORKS

Universal and innovative, the architect Antoni Gaudí left behind an architectonic legacy that still captivates today for the originality of its technical and aesthetic resources.

Finca Güell
Located in Barcelona, it was the first commission from Eusebi Güell.

Casa Vicens
Clearly of Mudéjar inspiration, it is one of Gaudí's first works.

Temple of the Sagrada Familia
Considered as Gaudí's most outstanding work, to which he dedicated more than 43 years of his life from 1883 until 1926.

| 1883 | 1884 | 1886 | 1888 | 1889 | 1890 | 1892 |

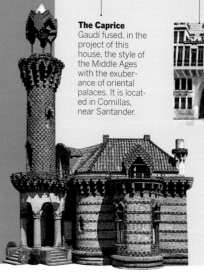

The Caprice
Gaudí fused, in the project of this house, the style of the Middle Ages with the exuberance of oriental palaces. It is located in Comillas, near Santander.

Güell Palace
Situated in the heart of Barcelona, it is a work of great sobriety.

Casa de los Botines
Located in León, this building is a clear exponent of Gaudí's Gothic period.

Teresian College
Plans the lecture rooms for the college situated in Barcelona.

Park Güell
Constructed between 1900 and 1914, it was devised as a garden city project. Gaudí knew how to integrate the architectonic, decorative elements along with nature. In the year 1984 UNESCO declared the park a World Heritage Site.

Casa Batlló
It is an exceptional example of Gaudí's organic architecture. On its façade, the balconies appear to hang like bird nests.

La Pedrera
Built between 1906 and 1912, it is another of Gaudí's masterpieces, which stands out for its sinuous façade and chimneys on the terrace roof.

| 1893 | 1895 | 1898 | 1900 | 1904 | 1906 | 1914 |

The Güell wine cellars
Were built in the locality of Garraf.

Torre Bellesguard
In this house, Gaudí wanted to recall the glorious past of Catalonia in the Middle Ages.

Casa Calvet
Gaudí gave it a refined and sober style. It received the prize from the City Council for the best building of 1900.

Episcopal palace
The residence of the Bishop of Astorga (León) is in keeping with the neo-gothic style.

Güell Colony church
Only the crypt was built, to which Gaudí applied numerous technical innovations.

02

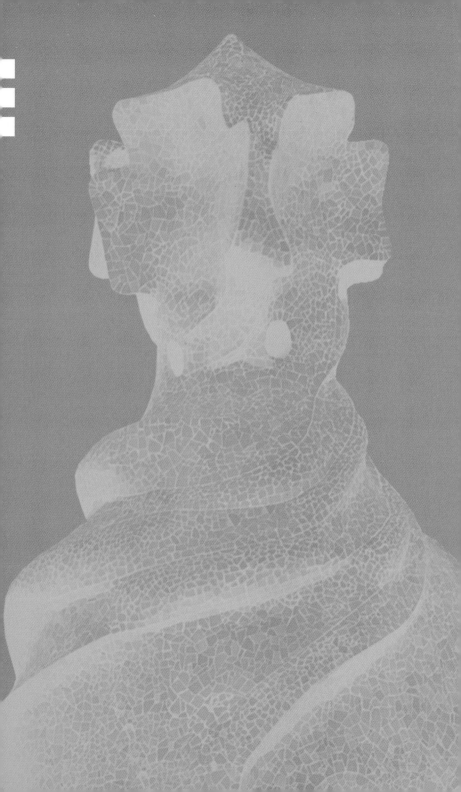

GAUDÍ'S PROJECT

Architecture in motion

Antoni Gaudí's passion for the changing balance of nature is manifested in La Pedrera.

The influence of the natural world in Antoni Gaudí's architecture is found in practically all of his works. However, it was in Casa Milà, popularly known as La Pedrera for its resemblance to a quarry, when he could give expression to all its exuberance. His last civil work combines the mutability and perfection of nature in each and every one of its elements. Combining the most advanced of engineering and the most daring of aesthetic freedom, Gaudí raised a building, totally undulating and throbbing like a living being, an architectonic sculpture which would become one of the most influential and controversial monuments of the 20th century. Situated on Passeig de Gràcia, the most important avenue at that time, an imposing rocky massif was erected, which in the sunlight appears to move like the waves in the sea or the dunes in the desert. Over this architectonic landscape, elements such as the chimneys on the terrace roof or the balcony railings recall animals and vegetables in constant metamorphosis. What is more, the architect didn't just limit the use of curved forms and plays of light to be simple decorative elements, but in the interior he used them to give functionalism to a building designed for the renting out of apartments. Likewise, around the two large interior patios, which illuminate and distribute the rooms, Gaudí devised an original structure with columns and beams that, by not having load-bearing walls, permitted the free distribution of space.

Antoni Gaudí around 1878

The nature of stone

A work ahead of its time. Casa Milà was considered as a building out of tune with Passeig de Gràcia. The boldness of its striking organic shapes aroused all types of reactions.

A new way of understanding architecture

With the commission of Casa Milà, Gaudí gave free rein to his imagination when tackling the project of a corner building in the Eixample. Passeig de Gràcia had become the neuralgic centre of the bourgeoisie and its distinguished families entrusted their homes there to prestigious architects. However, once finished, La Pedrera supposed a rupture not only with the aesthetics of the period, but also with the technical innovations of his colleagues of his generation. With its giant sculptural appearance, it became one of the most striking and controversial buildings in Barcelona.

 DATA
A POLEMIC BUILDING

La Pedrera generated controversial opinions amongst the Barcelonans. This was how the publications of the period reflected public feeling with illustrations depicting it as a cave of vermin, the aftermath of an earthquake or a parking area for airships.

STAIRWELLS
They connect the attic with the terrace. All are topped with crosses.

SENTRY PASS
With four cupolas, it allows one to skirt around the façade.

INTERIOR PATIO
These openings guarantee ventilation and the luminosity of all floors.

TERRACE ROOF

PASSEIG DE GRÀCIA FAÇADE

MAIN ENTRANCE
Leads into the vestibule, where the access ways to the apartments start.

CHAMFERED CORNER FAÇADE

Drawing
A parody of the poster of the opera *Twilight of the Gods* by Wagner, where an epic Gaudí is shown directing the construction work.

Antoni Gaudí

" The projecting elements must be combined with the recesses, in such a way that each convex element, which is placed in full light, puts the other in shadow..."

CHIMNEYS
The shape of their cowls resembles owls or African masks.

Natural influence

Antoni Gaudí devised the Casa Milà to imitate nature. If in the interior structure the adaptability of living beings is emulated, then the exterior reflects their movements. With its unusual curves, the building undulates like a natural landscape. However, the architect is believed to have been inspired by some concrete reference, although this hypothesis has never been confirmed. Given the great evocative power of the work, the theories about the sources of inspiration for La Pedrera are infinite.

Mountains. The rocky formations of Capadocia and the massif of Montserrat are the most quoted.

Sea. The façade seems like a rough sea, as in the drawings of the Japanese Hokusai, in fashion at the time.

FAÇADE ON PROVENÇA STREET

Desert. The sinuous edges of the building are dune-like, changing at will in the wind.

MAIN FLOOR
As was the custom, the main floor would be taken over by the owners of the property, the Milàs.

GROUND FLOOR
Built for businesses. The first was a tailor's, which opened in 1928.

BALCONIES
In combination with the waving forms, their irregular railings are plant-like.

A monumental building

The synthesis of the Gaudian universe.

La Pedrera was conceived as a monumental building that combines maximum rationality and structural rigour with an unlimited artistic and creative liberty.

In search of light

One of the most original aspects of Gaudí's project was the search for light in all areas, given that, in the properties of the time, interior spaces were dark. He therefore organized the ground plan starting from two large central patios that were transformed into the axis of the project, because, apart from providing light and ventilation, they also combined access from the outside and vertical movement. Positioning the rooms and bedrooms towards the street and the service areas towards the inner patios, Gaudí made sure that all the rooms were well illuminated and ventilated.

Catenary arches of the attic

Chimneys
The terrace roof has 30 outlets for smoke, all of them with an unusual and enigmatic sculpted appearance.

+12.000
METRES SQUARE
Is the total surface area that all the floors of La Pedrera take up.

1.323
METRES SQUARE
Is the area taken up by each floor, without counting the interior patios.

84,60
METRES OF FAÇADES
Divided into three stretches, unified by undulating horizontal lines.

33
BALCONIES
Are distributed on the façades, each one of different shape and size.

APARTMENTS
Each floor destined for rented flats is divided up into 3 or 4 apartments.

21,15

PATIO
Distributes the entrances and illuminates the interior rooms of the apartments.

SHOPS
From the year 1928 the exterior perimeter of the ground floor is used for shops.

ACCESS RAMP
Joins the basement with the patio, where the vehicles come in directly off the street.

GARAGE
Devised as car park and stables, the basement is adapted for automobiles, now common amongst the city's bourgeoisie.

The Milàs' staircase. The two interior patios have staircases leading exclusively to the main floor reserved for the owners of the property: Mrs Roser Segimon i Artells and Mr Pere Milà i Camps.

Patios

TERRACE ROOF

Attic

FOURTH FLOOR

Secondary staircase

Access to the flat

43,35 m

20,10 m

GROUND FLOOR

Secondary staircase

Main staircase

Access via Provença Street

Access via Passeig de Gràcia

BASEMENT

Auditory constructed in the refurbishment of 1994.

The layout of the building

Ahead of his time, in the basement of La Pedrera, Gaudí created one of the first garages in Barcelona for automobiles. Above it, he reserved the ground floor for the interior patios and the entrances. The following five floors were set aside for apartments; the main floor for the owners and the rest for rent. He topped the monument with communal spaces: an attic for laundry and lumber rooms and, above this, the terrace roof.

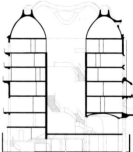

First studies of Gaudí. In the plans of 1906, the main staircase arrived at all floors.

DATA
A VERY LARGE HOUSE

PERMITTED HEIGHT

La Pedrera greatly exceeded the height and volume permitted in the Eixample for the municipal ordinances of the period. For this reason, the City Council threatened a hefty fine if the extra floors weren't demolished. In the end, all was resolved on recognition of the exceptional character of the building in 1909.

The structure

An organic work. *Gaudí conceived La Pedrera as a living organism in constant movement, whose structure could be easily adapted for future requirements.*

A skeleton without walls

Faced with the challenge of designing a building of rented apartments, Gaudí opted for an original structure on which all the dividing partitions of apartments and rooms could be eliminated and repositioned according to the necessities of the owners and tenants. This was possible due to the fact that there wasn't a master load-bearing wall. A simple and ingenious framework of pillars, columns and beams sustains all the weight of the building. An innovative solution that converts each floor into an open-plan space.

Columns
The majority are cylindrical, after testing proved this shape provided greater resistance.

Girders
Interweaving, make space for the wrought iron that supports the ceilings and floors.

Self-supporting façade
It is supported by its own structure and is joined to the building by means of curved girders. For this reason it can have this peculiar undulating shape.

FAÇADE

 DATA
FROM ANTONI GAUDÍ TO LE CORBUSIER

Open-plan
The structure of La Pedrera was more than 20 years ahead of its time. In 1931, the Swiss architect, Le Corbusier designed the Villa Savoye in France on an open-plan basis, a very similar concept to the one used by Gaudí.

Le Corbusier
The Swiss architect was a great admirer of Gaudí, whose works he visited in 1928.

+250
COLUMNS
make up the skeleton of the building. Of irregular distribution and variable width. There are just ninety of them in the basement alone.

50
CENTIMETRES
depth was enough to dig the foundations, thanks to the extreme hardness of the clay floor.

40
TONNES
is the weight of the iron girders used on each floor. In order to raise the girders a crane was invented for the occasion.

 Antoni Gaudí

Architecture creates the organism and therefore this must have a law in consonance with nature"

Naval engineering. The complex curved girders, which unite the façade with the structure of the floors, were produced in the shipyards of Barceloneta with the presses used to make the hulls of boats.

Past and present

In order to erect the structure of Casa Milà, Gaudí combined traditional stone and brick with the modernity of iron. The latter was used for all the girders and tie-beams of the ceilings and floors. In the columns, in contrast, he alternated the three materials. For those that supported greater weight, cast iron, which had burst into architecture a few decades before. For those within sight, on the main floor and the patios, stone. For the rest, brick, which went back a long way in Catalan construction.

The attic of Casa Milà
It was built with 270 brick catenary arches. An undulating system that set it apart from the rest of the floors in the property.

Attic. In the middle of construction, they had to finish the ceiling.

01. La Pedrera in 1918. Of monumental appearance, Casa Milà became the most striking building on Passeig de Gràcia, the most important avenue of the period. **02. Sentry walk.** Situated on the upper part of the façades and with sinuous curves, it skirts the entire perimeter of the building. **03. Ceilings.** Show great unevenness and undulations inspired by whirlpools. **04. Railings.** The balconies have recycled wrought iron railings, designed by Gaudí and architect Jujol. **05. Patio on Provença Street.** Stands out for its large size and its more than 150 metres square surface. **06. Terrace.** View from the terrace roof, where one can appreciate the different elements that make it up.

03

THE FAÇADES

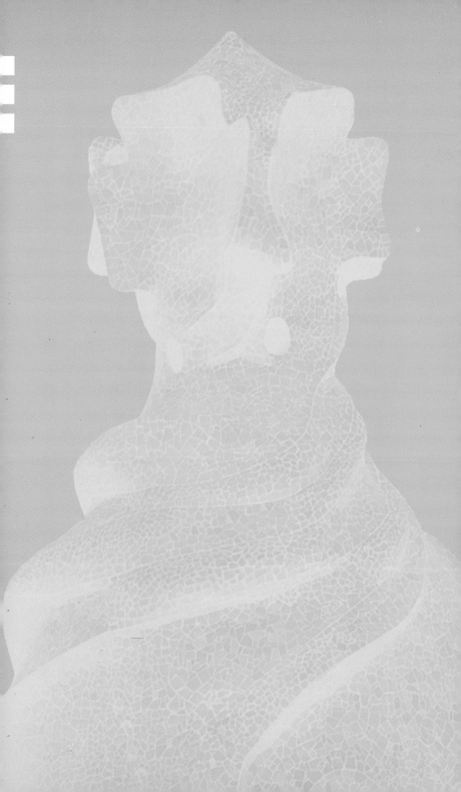

In motion. A continuous horizontal serpentine line marks out each floor of the building.

THE FAÇADES

An architectonic sculpture

Gaudí bestows great movement on the three façades of the Casa Milà and endows them with a sculptural value.

Like a sea of stone, La Pedrera's façades seem to be constantly moving. Their fluid and undulating forms, receding or projecting, means that the way they are perceived will change according to the sunlight or the position of the observer. Gaudí managed to convey vivacity, tension and dynamism, lending plasticity to a material as robust as stone whilst combining it with evocative recycled iron railings. At the age of 54, Gaudí possessed his own style, free from other historic trends, which allowed him to plan the façades of his last civil work as innovative and groundbreaking work. The architect looks for and achieves a greater structural and stylistic freedom than in other works, letting his imagination loose and, as synthesis of his architectonic evolution, he creates organic façades of great provocative power, which have been subject to all types of interpretations through the course of time. This is how the idea of the giant wave surged, a cliff, a mountain, a desert, a fist, or from a more metaphysical perspective, it is a metaphor for the flow of life. The passion and creativity Antoni Gaudí channelled into the arrangements of the façades of La Pedrera exceeded the limits of architecture, transforming a house of neighbours into a remarkable sculptural work.

The railings are a move towards abstract sculpture.

The façades
Stone and light in constant motion

On the façades, Gaudí shapes the stone and iron imprinting them with a plastic and expressive treatment. With the use of light and shadow he manages a greater sensation of movement and thus creates a unique mass; forceful, charged with vitality and dynamism. The wrought iron railings enclosing the balconies, considered to be a precedent of contemporary abstract sculpture, enrich its artistic value.

The façades

La Pedrera possess three façades: one on Passeig de Gràcia, one on the chamfered corner and one on Provença Street. All of them unite robustness and dynamism, two concepts that in principle are conflicting, but are combined by harmonizing the solidity of the stone with the fluidity of the undulations, the sinuousness of the balconies and the irregularity of the 150 windows. Measuring 30 metres high, the façades' 84 metre long extension is distributed in an unequal way. The longest façade of 43.45 metres is found on Provença Street, while the other two occupy around 20 metres each. The monument is seen to be unified by means of horizontal sequences that are situated between each one of the floors.

The three façades
If stretched out in a straight line, the façade of Passeig de Gràcia, the corner one and the one on Provença Street would measure 84.60 metres long.

150 WINDOWS
different in shape and size, are found on the three exterior façades. Some windows are divided into two or three sections, with this irregularity generating a greater dynamism.

PASSEIG DE GRÀCIA FAÇADE

CHAMFERE CORNER FAÇADE

The first idea. The original project of 1906 sketched out very similar solutions to those carried out on the Casa Batlló. Pere Milà fell in love with this house and for this reason decided to contract Gaudí as the Pedrera's architect.

Casa Batlló, 1904 - 1906

The irrigation system

Gaudí wanted iron and vegetation to mix within the stone balconies; so he planned an original and avant-garde automatic irrigation system, which was never to be installed.

Material and colour

The façades are constructed with stone from Vilafranca del Penedès and Garraf. Their characteristic creamy, white colour undergoes constant mutations, whether it is throughout the day or during the different seasons of the year. These changes are due to the varying positions of the sun that, along with the texture of the stone, generates a sensation of movement.

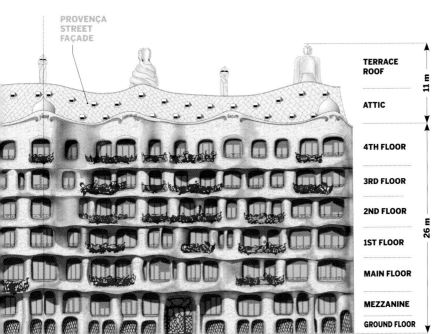

PROVENÇA STREET FAÇADE

TERRACE ROOF	11 m
ATTIC	
4TH FLOOR	
3RD FLOOR	
2ND FLOOR	
1ST FLOOR	26 m
MAIN FLOOR	
MEZZANINE	
GROUND FLOOR	

The rear façade

Gaudí projected the façade that looks out onto the block interior courtyard with similar undulations to the other façades, but with greater sobriety. Organized in continuous terraces, which go in and out, each floor generates sinuous bands on which the iron railings form a rhomboid weave.

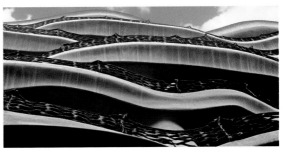

Rear façade. Undulated, it is done in brick that is rendered over.

Passeig de Gràcia façade

In contrast with the classical buildings on the avenue, Gaudí plans the most placid of the three façades and accords it gentle undulations.

In the heart of the city

On Passeig de Gràcia, the most prestigious artery of Barcelona when work on Casa Milà commences, Gaudí plans one of the three façades. Of serene appearance and extending 21,15 metres, its frieze is topped with the word *Ave* and it is the only façade lacking a main entrance. Its energetic walls, in combination with its gentle undulations, are integrated within the formal unit of the monument in a simple and natural way.

The water lilies. Placed high up on the façade, the water lilies symbolize the purity of the Virgin Mary.

The windows
They get smaller towards the upper floors to offset the quantity of light that they receive.

Iron railings
Despite their solidness and thickness, their shapes are very gentle.

1907
THE DENOUNCED COLUMN

A municipal inspector complained because one column invaded the pavement on Passeig de Gràcia; Gaudí threatened to cut it off inscribing: "Column mutilated by order of City Council".

DATA
THE FIRST SHOP

The Mosella tailor's shop
In 1928, the Milà family decides to put the ground floor areas up for rent to businesses. The first to set up on Passeig de Gràcia is Mosella tailor's shop. Its clients include the artist Salvador Dalí, an admirer of La Pedrera.

The architect Josep Maria Jujol
Guided by Gaudí, he designed some of the balcony railings. Their complex structures were forged with metal scrap.

33 RAILINGS sculpted, all of them different, are placed on the balconies and galleries.

LOCATION

Catalonia. The four bars of the Catalan coat of arms can be identified between the abstract shapes of the railings.

The dove. Placed on the first wrought iron balcony of the façade, it was supervised directly by Gaudí.

The mask. Situated high up on the façade, it appears to represent a Greek theatre mask.

The railings

In the arrangement of the façades, the iron railings act as a decorative element and contrast with the stone. Made from recycled scrap, the railings are an artistic jumble of bars, sheets, screws and other elements. They were produced in the workshops owned by the Badia brothers in Barcelona under Gaudí's strict guidance and with the collaboration of a young architect, Jujol. The railings, like sculptural collages, are all different, but follow the same concept and treatment. They are revolutionary works that transcend craftwork converting into works of art and are considered as one of the first abstract sculptures.

The sea. The façades evoke the sea and the twisting iron of the railings resembles seaweed.

Chamfered corner façade

Monumental and austere, La Pedrera's most projecting façade has one of the entranceways and the main gallery.

The capital
Placed next to the entranceway and carved in stone, it repeats the play of shadows and undulations on the façade.

An original gallery

In the junction of Passeig de Gràcia and Provença Street, emerges La Pedrera's central and most outstanding façade. One of the two entranceways is found here and over it hangs the gallery on the main floor, which is the most important floor in the house, in which its promoters, the Milà family, resided. Forming a unique body, the entranceway and the gallery window are joined together by means of two solid lateral stone pillars, partly joined to the façade and partly separate from it, which invade the pavement as if they were two great elephant legs. Antoni Gaudí plans the integration of the entranceway with the main gallery inspired by the work of a baroque architect, *madrilène* Pedro de Ribera, whom he greatly admired.

Façade
Facing the southeast and measuring 20 metres high, the chamfered corner façade has one of the two entranceways to the building.

1984
WAS THE YEAR
in which UNESCO declared Casa Milà a World Heritage Site, in recognition of the exceptional creative contribution that Gaudí made to 20th century architecture.

Balconies. The glazed floor of some of the balconies facilitated the entry of light to the chamfered corner entranceway.

The skylight. Situated on the balcony floor that overhangs the main floor, it filters light through to the gallery.

The shell. It is found on the upper part of the gallery of the main floor; often a pilgrim symbol.

Carles Mani
The sculptor, contracted by Antoni Gaudí for the Sagrada Familia, also collaborated on La Pedrera carrying out the sculpture of the Virgin, which was never put into position.

LOCATION

The letter "M". Situated on the upper part of the façade, a letter *M* carved in stone represents Mary.

The rose
The rose engraved high up on the façade alludes to the Virgin of the Rosary and is a reference to the owner's name.

Mary
Positioned in the centre of the image, she alludes to the Virgin of Gràcia, Patron Saint of this town.

The sculpture of Mary

Gaudí planned that a sculpture of the Virgin with Baby Jesus would crown the chamfered corner façade. He therefore entrusted Carles Mani to sculpt this work, more than 4 metres high, and to include the archangels Saint Michael and Saint Gabriel just as they appear in Revelations. However, the image was never cast in bronze nor put into position as, according to various versions, it didn't satisfy Pere Milà and, according to others, was suspended due to the riots of *Semana Tràgica* in Barcelona in 1909, when anarchist groups set fire to numerous buildings with religious symbols.

The base of the sculpture
According to a false myth of the period, La Pedrera was just the pedestal to sustain the colossal sculpture of the Virgin.

The location. The Virgin had to be positioned in the middle of the upper part of the chamfered corner façade.

Provença façade

Of huge size and great dynamism, its undulations appear to have been moulded from clay.

The windows
They included a wooden roller blind system, a novelty in its time. The present ones are made of aluminium.

The longest façade. Measuring 43.35 metres long, its undulating rhythm seems to be moulded by hand.

An undulating wall

The façade that is situated on Provença Street has one of the two entranceways to the house and offers a play of waves and movement more accentuated and vibrant than the other two façades. Antoní Gaudí considered that the balconies had to jut out more to create shadows that would at the same time protect the residences, as due to its position this is the façade that receives more sunlight. Thanks to its 43.35 metres width, it is the widest of the three façades and the façade possessing the most balconies and wrought iron railings.

Provença Street entranceway
Of organic forms, it combines stone, wrought iron and glass.

The numeration
By occupying a corner plot, La Pedrera has entranceways leading out on to two streets. On Provença Street it is numbered 261.

43
METRES
is the width of the façade located on Provença Street, the largest of the three.

The phrase on the façades
On the frieze of the façades are words in Latin from the Angelus greeting, *Ave Gratia M Plena Dominus Tecum,* carved with the typical writing of architect Jujol. Gaudí wanted to give a special significance to the building, as it is with this phrase that the Ave María prayer begins: "Hail, Mary, full of grace, the Lord is with thee".

The phrase. *Ave - Gratia - M - Plena - Dominus - Tecum,* on the frieze on the façade.

The restoration
In the eighties, La Pedrera was a house that was dark, dirtied by pollution and mouldy, showing signs of deterioration such as fissures, cracks and rust within its iron structures. The situation changed in 1986 when its new owner, Caixa de Catalunya, starts upon its cleaning and restoration.

1986
THE FAÇADES
are restored when Caixa de Catalunya acquires the house. This work, which finishes in 1989, constitutes the first phase of a restoration project of the entire building.

RESTORATION
THE FAÇADE RECUPERATES ITS SPLENDOUR

Before. The railings were rusty with the risk of falling fragments.

After. They fixed the loose elements; rust was eliminated and then painted.

The façades before the restoration process

Before. The stone was stained with soot, rust and fissures.

After. With treatment, the stone recuperates its original colour.

The construction

Antoni Gaudí planned self-supporting façades and transformed the stone into a plastic and expressive material.

The chipping of the stone
As if it were an enormous sculpture, numerous stonemasons chiselled the stone on the façade.

Independent façades

Gaudí builds the façades of independent form in relation to the structure of the building. This way, he achieves a great formal liberty that allows him to plan undulating walls with numerous windows. In order to design the shape of the façades, he works on a plaster model at a scale of 1:10. Once finished, he cuts the model into various fragments which are taken to the construction, where the stonemasons use them as models to carve the stones at different points on the façades.

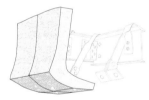

Structure. The façade stones are supported by iron beams.

 DATA
THE CONSTRUCTOR OF LA PEDRERA

The building contractor of La Pedrera, who had already worked with Gaudí on previous projects, was almost ruined building the façade, because some stones had to be raised almost four times before being put correctly into place. In the end, Gaudí verified the veracity of Josep Bayó's complaints and got Pere Milà to increase the money destined for the façade.

Josep Bayó Font

Bayó's crane. The constructor of La Pedrera invented a special metal crane to raise the blocks of stones for the façades.

The locomobile
In order to transport the stones from the quarries to Barcelona, a kind of steamroller called the *Locomóvil Ruston* was used.

Antoni Gaudí

I have tired a lot those who work with me, for never have I considered things to be well done until convincing myself that they can't be perfected any more"

Uncarved façade
In 1910 the canvas covering the façade during construction work was removed: the stones were now positioned, but the arrises and curves were yet to be done.

4.500
BLOCKS OF STONE
is the approximate quantity of ashlars that the façades were built with.

Undulations. The façades present a delicate play of undulations thanks to the careful chiselling of the stone, done as if it were a sculpture.

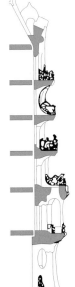

The finishing touches
The façades were built under the meticulous management of Gaudí, who didn't let any detail go to chance. Once the blocks of stone had been chiselled and put into place, the architect personally controlled the final adjustments and the labour of the stonemasons in order that the undulations, receding or projecting, were perfectly adjusted to the project.

Self-supporting façade
As it didn't function as a load-bearing wall, it could be lighter and slender.

Plaster model
Apparently, Gaudí produced two models of La Pedrera: one to guide the final adjustment of the façades and the second for exhibition at the Universal Exhibition in Paris of 1910.

THE FAÇADE RAILINGS

The expressive wrought iron railings reveal Gaudí's great artistic freedom, anticipating abstract sculpture.

Gaudí
The architect designed the first railing in the Badier workshop and Jujol developed the rest under his guidance.

1

Provença railings
They stand out for their larger size, proportional to the balconies, and their open forms, lighter and more porous than those on the other façades.

Size
Their large size is appreciated when comparing them with a man measuring 1.80 metres.

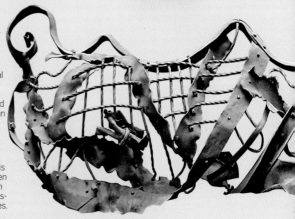

2

Chamfered corner's railings
Of smaller size, these railings are distinguished for the union of larger more compact pieces that create a dense, solid effect.

RECYCLED IRON
Gaudí chose, from amongst the metal scrap, the pieces and elements that he could recycle and combine.

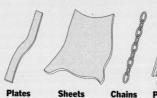

Plates   **Sheets**   **Chains**   **Profiles**   **Mesh**   **Tubes**

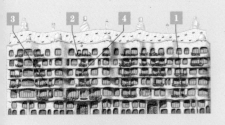

MOCKERY
The balcony railings didn't escape the irony of the time. They were compared with a cod stall or a train crash.

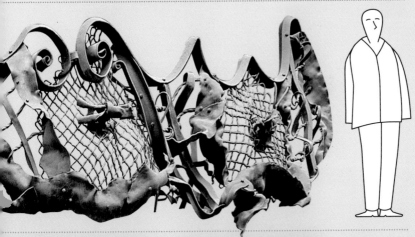

33
RAILINGS
span the extension of the façades.

4.100
SCREWS
is the approximate number of screws and rivets used to unite the railings.

Mask. On one of the railings the profile of a mask can be made out, similar to those used on Casa Batlló.

Star and flower. Natural details abound, like a flower with its petals and a six-pointed star in relief.

UNION OF PIECES
The different elements of recycled iron that make up a railing are joined with screws or rivets.

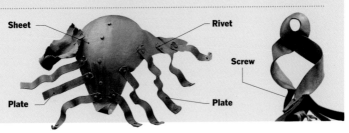

Sheet

Rivet

Screw

Plate

Plate

01. Skylight. Some balconies and terraces have a translucent glazed floor that lets light through.
02, 03 y 04. Railings. Different details of the artistic work carried out by Jujol and Gaudí, joining recycled iron pieces. **05. Undulations.** The façade on Provença Street is where the play of receding and projecting elements is most emphasized. **06. Columns.** On the ground floor, the columns have greater relief than on the other floors of the building. **07. *Tecum.*** This word is carved high up on the Provença Street façade, completing the Angelus, written in Latin. **08. Carving.** The curved forms of the façades were achieved by chiselling away at the stone, one by one, under Gaudí's guidance.

04

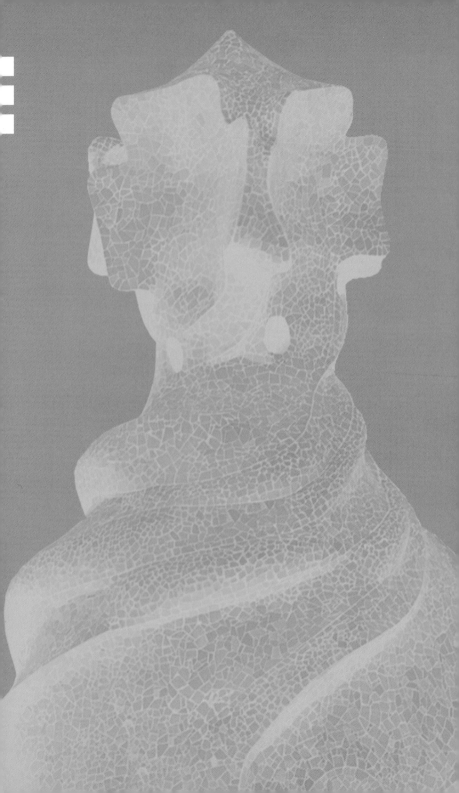

Entrance on Passeig de Gràcia. The staircase leading up to the main floor goes round the interior patio.

THE ENTRANCEWAYS

Innovation and fluidity

Gaudí devises a harmonious and natural communication between the exterior, the vestibules and the interior patios.

Gaudí devised an agile and dynamic architecture for the entrance floor of La Pedrera that meant that the passing from one space to the next would be fluid and natural. He therefore designed two great entranceways, worked in wrought iron and glass, which allow viewing of the interior and facilitate communication with the exterior. Once inside the house, the vestibules and the wide patios act as areas of transition between the streets and the residences. The architect organized all the ground floor around the two central patios, which were planned with the objective of providing natural light and ventilation to the residences and, at the same time, brought together the transit that connects the different floors of the building. But, without a doubt, one of the most revolutionary concepts for the time, was to use lifts as the main means of access to the residences, leaving the stairs as auxiliary and service accessways. However, this was not the only innovation that Gaudí introduced into the Pedrera. The other great novelty was the design of the underground car park, one of the first in the city, which the vehicles accessed, without obstacles, from the street by crossing vestibules and patios and by going down a spacious ramp until the parking space that each neighbour had at his disposition.

Capital and shaft. Done in stone and with organic shapes.

The entrance floor

A new concept to access the residences

The doorways and shops, fitted out from 1928, are the external face of the ground floor. Once inside the house, Gaudí planned the lifts as the principal means of access to the rented properties, reserving the stairs as a service staircase, quite innovative for the time. For the main floor, the architect designed the two monumental staircases, one in each of the patios, decorated with plants and painted murals.

An original distribution

On the ground floor, Gaudí planned an original and integrated distribution, combining aesthetics and functional use. That is how, entering by any of the two doorways, we find ourselves with a vestibule that is in charge of organizing access to the residences. The two large patios are used for the transit of automobiles, where once inside one can manoeuvre to go out again or go down to the basement garage. To emphasize the idea of a fluid communication, Gaudí linked up the two entranceways with interior pavements that went around the entire floor.

Passeig de Gràcia patio
Of circular ground plan, it is connected with the patio on Provença Street by means of a passageway.

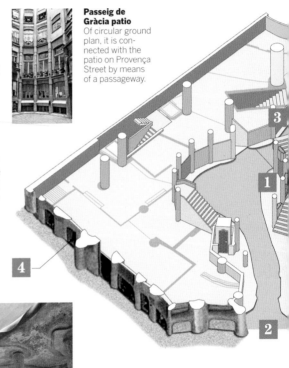

The main staircase. Winding around the patio of Passeig de Gràcia, the staircase leading up to the residence of the Milà family is decorated with paintings and plants.

DATA
THE GRILLES ON THE GROUND FLOOR

Originally, all the openings on the ground floors had grilles, which were then removed when the shops were set up. A collector bought one of them for 60,000 dollars. At present, this grille is conserved in the MoMA museum of New York.

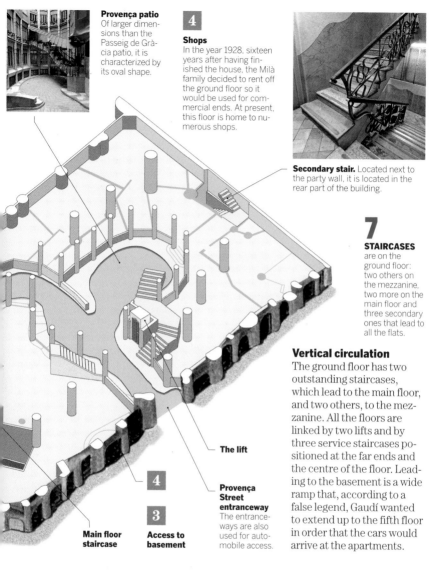

Provença patio
Of larger dimensions than the Passeig de Gràcia patio, it is characterized by its oval shape.

Shops
In the year 1928, sixteen years after having finished the house, the Milà family decided to rent off the ground floor so it would be used for commercial ends. At present, this floor is home to numerous shops.

Secondary stair. Located next to the party wall, it is located in the rear part of the building.

7
STAIRCASES
are on the ground floor: two others on the mezzanine, two more on the main floor and three secondary ones that lead to all the flats.

Vertical circulation
The ground floor has two outstanding staircases, which lead to the main floor, and two others, to the mezzanine. All the floors are linked by two lifts and by three service staircases positioned at the far ends and the centre of the floor. Leading to the basement is a wide ramp that, according to a false legend, Gaudí wanted to extend up to the fifth floor in order that the cars would arrive at the apartments.

The lift

4

Provença Street entranceway
The entranceways are also used for automobile access.

3

Main floor staircase

Access to basement

2

Passeig de Gràcia entranceway
Its doors combine glass panes and iron, allowing light to filter through to the vestibules. Its structure functions as a security gate.

Porter's lodge
Located in the vestibule, next to the porter's residence, it is made of iron and cut glass with natural floral motifs.

Passeig de Gràcia vestibule

A space of transition which links the outside with the inside, organizing the traffic flow to the different corners of the building.

The distributor

This vestibule is a large space delimited by stone columns and an undulating ceiling, comparable to a grotto. Its function is to organize the access to the different flats. From here emerge the staircases to the main floor and the mezzanine, the same way as one of the service staircases that, along with the lift, link all floors.

1993
IS THE YEAR that the first restoration of the arrangement of painted murals that decorate the vestibules was completed. This work had been started in 1991.

Patio, stair and vestibule

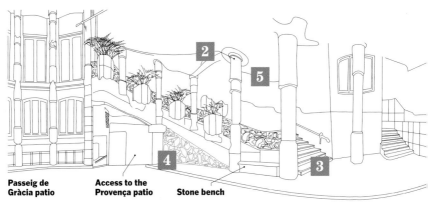

Passeig de Gràcia patio

Access to the Provença patio

Stone bench

To the basement. The ramp that goes down commences from the passageway that links the two patios.

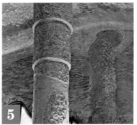

Reflection. On the main staircase, opposite one of the stone columns, there are other columns painted on the wall.

Details. On the columns of the vestibule are decorative engravings of helicoidal organic shape.

1

Lamp
Its wrought iron and glass design harmonizes with the style and aesthetics of the doorway.

2

Column
Of naturalist shape, the stone of the capital blends into the paintings on the ceiling.

LOCATION

The grilles
Executed in wrought iron, the staircase banisters combine undulated shapes of varying style and size.

3

The Milà staircase
On each one of the two vestibules, Gaudí placed a staircase of great dimensions, decorated with painted murals and vegetation, which led up to the residence of the promoters, the Milà family.

The staircases

As is often the case in Gaudí's works, the staircases in the Pedrera do not follow straight lines nor adopt smooth surfaces. On the contrary, they prefer changing runs and curved steps. The most striking of the staircases is the one that, from the vestibule, leads directly and exclusively to the main floor.

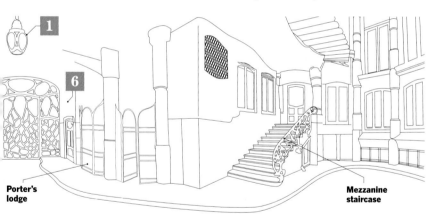

Porter's lodge

Mezzanine staircase

Pictorial decoration

The whole vestibule is oil-painted with different mythological and floral motifs. Some of these walls are influenced by 16th century tapestries where the poet Ovidio's *The Metamorphosis* is represented. These paintings help us to understand the ideas that Gaudí devised for the Pedrera.

Pan the mythological God and a nymph

RESTORATION
COLOUR RETURNS TO THE PAINTINGS

Restorer of the Sistine Chapel, Don Gianluigi Colalucci, carried out the initial study in order to restore the painted murals.

Provença vestibule

Gaudí decorated the walls and ceilings with painted murals charged with symbolism and numerous artisanal contributions.

A fluid entranceway

Of similar morphology and function to that on Passeig de Gràcia, its task is to distribute and organize access in this entranceway. It is therefore equipped with a lift, the mezzanine staircase and the main floor staircase. The vestibule also houses the porter's lodge and the wooden door of the porter's residence.

Main floor staircase

Provença Street patio

1 Door of the porter's residence

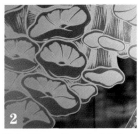

2 Water lilies on the porter's lodge

Arts and crafts

The vestibule shows numerous decorative details that reflect Gaudí's ideas. Works as diverse as the carved columns, the wrought iron on the staircases or the sculptural work on the doors manage a coherent formal unity in keeping with the architect's global vision.

Antoni Gaudí
The architect planned, for the vestibules, various painted murals whose themes were linked to the global symbolism of the house.

3

The lamp
Made only from wrought iron, it is of a different shape and size to the one on Passeig de Gràcia.

LOCATION

The painted murals

The Provença vestibule is also entirely decorated with mural representations. Some of these paintings allude to mythological stories, and others to the seven capital sins and to episodes of *Life is a Dream* by Calderón de la Barca, dramatist and classical poet of the Spanish Baroque.

**44
METRES
SQUARE**
is the area that Gaudí put aside for the vestibule, somewhat smaller than the one on Passeig de Gràcia, which is around 60 metres square.

4

The horse
On the wall of the entrance, a woman rides energetically on an enormous horse.

**Door on
Provença Street**

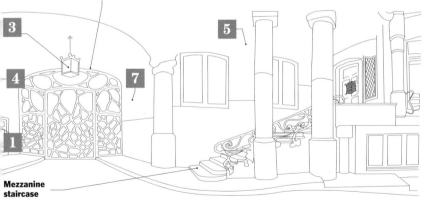

3

4

7

1

5

**Mezzanine
staircase**

5

Wrath. One of the painted murals dedicates a scene to wrath, the capital sin that condemns fury and anger.

6

Gluttony. A robust female figure represents gluttony, the sin for eating and drinking in excess.

7

Cassandra. Next to the entranceway, the prophetess Cassandra announces the destruction of Troy.

01. Decoration. The wall of the main staircase is decorated with a painting that depicts the vestibule columns. **02. Columns.** They join the ceiling by means of capitals of organic form. **03. The main floor staircase.** It is decorated with large plant pots placed between the columns and the railings. **04. Provença vestibule.** It has a surface area of 44 metres square and a height of 5 metres. **05. Accesses.** Next to the main entrance of the Provença vestibule is the door to the porter's residence, the main floor's staircase and the lift. **06. Mural.** The vestibules have painted murals of mythological character. **07. Railings.** The mezzanine staircase has a wrought iron railing with helicoidal shapes.

The patio system

Light reaches all floors by filtering through the interior patios around which revolve the residences.

The colour of the patios
Their paintings offer bold contrasts and free forms recalling the works of Jujol.

The importance of light

The interior of the Pedrera is structured around two spacious central patios that are interlinking, but have different shapes and dimensions. The one on Passeig de Gràcia, which is cylindrical, occupies a surface area of 90 metres square, while the one on Provença Street, of elliptic outline, measures 150 metres square. Gaudí designed them as a centre of communication, positioning the main floor and mezzanine staircases around its perimeter. Moreover, he organized the different spaces of the residences around these patios in order that they would receive ventilation and natural light.

Section
The cross section reveals the importance of the patios in the structure, the distribution and the functional nature of the building.

240
METRES SQUARE
is the total surface area of the two interior patios: 90 on Passeig de Gràcia and 150 on Provença.

Secondary ventilation well

Stairwell

Staircase to the mezzanine

Interior view of the Passeig de Gràcia patio. Of circular shape and large surface area, the patio owns numerous windows and is of one of the lungs of La Pedrera.

1

The staircase
Gaudí planned that the two staircases accessing the main floor would skirt the circumference of each one of the patios.

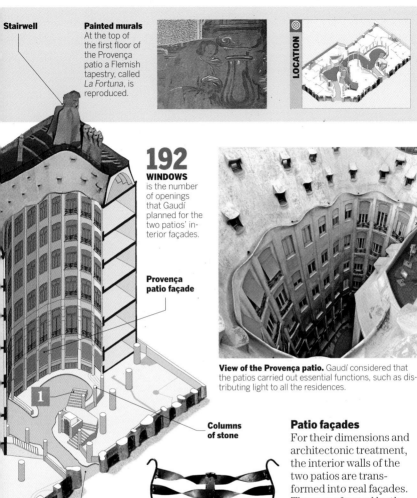

Stairwell

Painted murals
At the top of the first floor of the Provença patio a Flemish tapestry, called *La Fortuna*, is reproduced.

LOCATION

192
WINDOWS
is the number of openings that Gaudí planned for the two patios' interior façades.

Provença patio façade

View of the Provença patio. Gaudí considered that the patios carried out essential functions, such as distributing light to all the residences.

Columns of stone

The grilles. The wrought iron railings enclose and decorate the windows that look out on to the interior façades.

Provença Street vestibule

2

The windows
In order to obtain more natural light, Gaudí planned that the windows on the lower floors be of larger size than the higher ones.

Patio façades

For their dimensions and architectonic treatment, the interior walls of the two patios are transformed into real façades. These are formed by the sequence of cylindrical columns, of stone on the lower floors and rendered masonry on the upper ones, which emphasize a sensation of vertical movement. Full of windows and with special wrought iron railings, the walls are painted in yellow tones and decorated with pictorial murals of lively colour, some of which find inspiration in floral motifs and Flemish tapestries.

The basement floor

A parking area with direct access from the street

Located 4.69 metres below the level of Passeig de Gràcia, the basement floor was planned as a service area. In avant-garde style, Gaudí planned for it one of the first underground car parks of the city of Barcelona; which by means of a spacious ramp the vehicles could reach their parking space, situated below the patios, directly from the street.

The service zone

The basement floor was planned as a service zone, housing the garage, the lumber rooms and the machine room for the heating. Initially, Gaudí had thought about positioning the stables as he had done in Güell Palace, but on the wide spread use of the automobile, the basement of La Pedrera was converted into one of the first underground car parks. The cars could enter the building, by going down to the basement by a ramp, manoeuvring in a columnless zone and then park. Then there were the carport and lumber rooms for all the tenants. After, the secondary stairs united the basement with the remaining floors of the house.

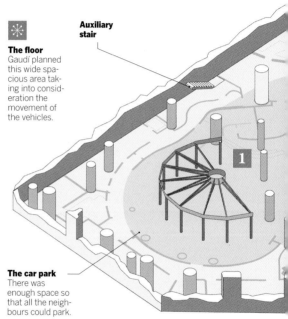

The floor
Gaudí planned this wide spacious area taking into consideration the movement of the vehicles.

Auxiliary stair

The car park
There was enough space so that all the neighbours could park.

1

DATA
THE AUTOMOBILE GARAGE

In order to satisfy the requirements of a tenant, whose Rolls Royce didn't have enough space to go around the garage ramp, Gaudí had to redo his sums and omit a pillar.

Rolls Royce

1

Bicycle wheel. To support the Passeig de Gràcia patio. Gaudí designed radial beams that formed a unique metallic structure, similar to a bicycle wheel.

ANECDOTE
In the Universal Exhibition of 1958, the Pavilion of the United States was greatly commented on for its originality, although it was similar to the bicycle wheel-like structure created by Gaudí.

90
COLUMNS
of iron, brick and stone support the building from the basement floor.

The auxiliary stair
On the basement floor there are two of them and they connect the garage with each one of the building's floors.

The auditorium. It is located in the same place where the carports and lumber rooms were.

250
PEOPLE
is the capacity of the auditorium inaugurated in 1994. It is accessed by the former car ramp and by a staircase that emerges from between the two patios.

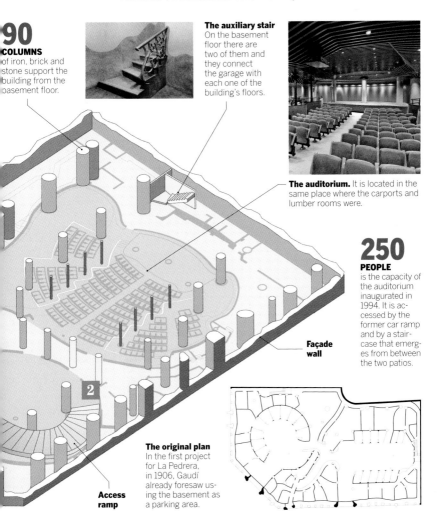

Façade wall

The original plan
In the first project for La Pedrera, in 1906, Gaudí already foresaw using the basement as a parking area.

Access ramp

Restoration of the basement floor
Concluded in 1994, the restoration of the basement floor transformed the former garage into an auditorium and a multi-purpose room. In this operation all the elements that weren't original and had been added with time were demolished, pillars were reinforced and the patio that corresponds to the rear façade was constructed.

Access ramp. Designed by Gaudí for vehicle access, it gets round a drop of 4.70 metres.

The shelter
As protection against the bombardments, during the Spanish Civil War, part of the basement was converted into a refuge strengthened with layers of cement rendered to the walls.

THE ENTRANCE DOORWAYS

The doorways of the two entrances, created in wrought iron and glass, stand out for their functional, innovative and thought-provoking design.

Door handle
Passeig de Gràcia doorway.

Light and protection

The doorways are planned to provide protection for the building, but without impeding communication with the outside. Therefore, Gaudí is inspired by natural forms, creating grilles that blend iron and glass, which act as an iron security grille while at the same time guarantee illumination of the vestibules. The architect designed the panes to be smaller in the lower part, where there is a higher risk of breakage, and larger ones in the upper part, where greater clarity is required.

Iron and glass
The combination of iron and glass was an aesthetic and functional solution at a time when great panes of glass weren't available.

Details
A series of marks are imprinted on the iron of the doors, which make them look like they've been carved with a soft material, almost finger modelled.

4,60
METRES
is the height of each one of the two wrought iron doors that lead into the building.

20
METRES SQUARE
is the approximate surface area of the glass on the doorways.

The functional nature of the doors
The central part of the doorways is used for the automobiles, while the lateral ones, for pedestrian access.

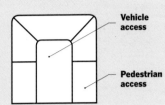

Vehicle access

Pedestrian access

Protection grille
On the doorways, the mesh of wrought iron, more closely woven on the lower level, also acts as security grille for the building.

The art of the abstract
Just like the façade railings, the doorways are considered precursors in the field of abstract art. They anticipate the style of the artists who, subsequently, converted wrought iron into a language of modern sculpture.

The Provença doorway. A light contrast between the Passeig de Gràcia and Provença doorways can be appreciated, given that in the latter the rounded forms are emphasized.

Nature as source of inspiration
The design of the doors appears to follow natural forms. According to varying hypotheses, they are based on a turtle shell, a butterfly's wings or cell tissue.

Turtle

Butterfly

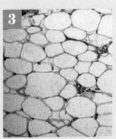

Cell tissue

01. Provença Street patio. It is the larger of the two, with oval shape and approximately 150 metres square. **02 y 08. Murals.** The patios are decorated with colourful paintings of floral motifs that have been deteriorating with time, although they can still be appreciated in some places. **03 y 07. Passeig de Gràcia patio.** Different views of the interior. **04. Windows.** Gaudí placed more than 190 windows on the patio walls in order that natural light would enter the flats. **05. Interior façade.** It measures 30 metres high and is formed by a series of stone columns on the lower part and rendered in the upper part. **06. Staircase.** Connects the patio with the mezzanine.

05

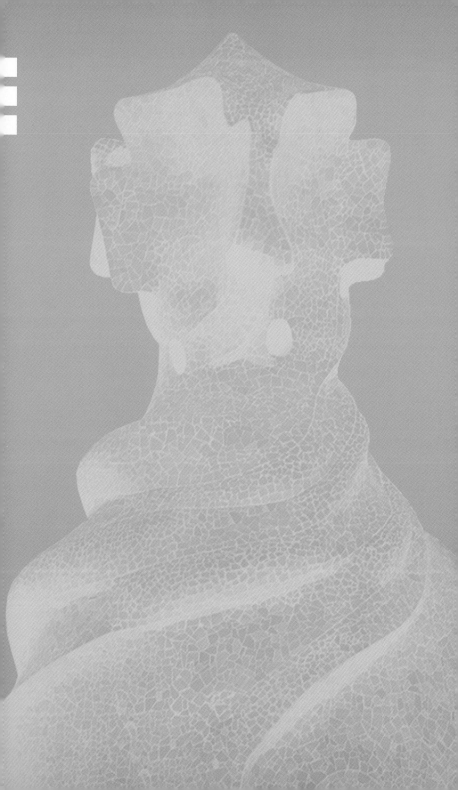

Wide spaces. The design of the structure of the Pedrera allows the elimination of load bearing walls.

THE APARTMENTS

The birth of the open-plan floor

Gaudí created a new concept of space that enabled him to vary the interior of the flats easily.

The floors of the flats in La Pedrera are organized around an innovative concept of space and way of understanding architecture: it happens to be the open-plan system, which Gaudí employs when building the flats and which is ahead of its time in construction methods. Thanks to this innovation, the entire house is supported by a structure of columns, girders and beams, metaphorically similar to a skeleton, which allows Gaudí to do away with load bearing walls and distribute the floors and the interiors of the flats with greater freedom and flexibility. In fact, all the floors had different layouts and all the flats offered a diversity and a variability that had been non-existent up until that time, as the walls of the flats not only could be positioned in any place, but could also be modified, moved and could change their function. Behind this innovation underlay a functional intention, given that Gaudí wanted to facilitate possible future transformations of the flats: in other words, that they could evolve and be adapted to the necessities of subsequent tenants and owners. This is what has happened on the main floor which, over the years, has been used for different purposes: first as a flat, later for offices, then as a bingo hall and, today, as an exhibition room.

Handle. Of curved shapes, the handles were designed by architect Jujol.

The main floor

A luxurious and spacious residence for the owners

The main floor was designed as the residence for the Milà family, the owners of the building. It constituted the largest home in the Pedrera that even doubled in size the most striking of the rented apartments. It could be directly accessed from the vestibules on Passeig de Gràcia and Provença Street by means of lifts or by the two monumental staircases that went around each of the patios and which only led to this apartment.

The Milàs' property

In the year 1911, the Milà family occupied the main floor, a year after work was completed on the building. This flat, measuring 1,323 metres square, has more than 35 areas that, entering by Passeig de Gràcia, were made up of: a hall that had an oratory and a reception room on either side; further along, Pere Milà's study; and then the dining room, the double bedroom and two bedrooms. Further down were more rooms and kitchen and toilets.

The flat in 1916
The Milàs decorated the house to their taste, following the neoclassical style of the period.

Handle. Designed to adapt to the hand.

The Provença staircase
The Milà's flat had two main entrances with individual staircases from the vestibules.

1911
The Milàs move into the house as soon as they receive permission from the Barcelona City Council.

1936
The family abandon the house due to the outbreak of the Spanish Civil War (1936-1939).

1939
The Milàs return to La Pedrera after Franco's troops enter the city of Barcelona.

1940
Pere Milà, the promoter, dies from a cancer that left him bedridden for six months.

Sculpted columns

Gaudí distributed fourteen stone columns in the Milàs' house, five of them carved with reliefs of different figures, signs, cuts and messages, whose design Josep Maria Jujol collaborated on. However, the owner, Roser Segimon, didn't agree with this style of decoration and decided to plaster over them in 1926, after Gaudí's death.

The zither. One of the columns shows a part of a zither or a harp with only three strings.

Engraved words. On another of the columns the words "forgive" and "forget" are inscribed in Catalan.

Main floor column

On one of the columns is a numerous decoration of reliefs of flowers, marine shapes and calligraphic inscriptions with words like: *charity*, *all*, *good*, *believe*, *forgive* and *forget*.

The rose
Situated on one of the columns on the main floor, it is one of the floral bas-reliefs that decorate the stone.

The reception room. It is entirely decorated with wooden furniture, designed by Gaudí, which allowed them to store objects in the cupboards and in the lidded benches.

1947
La Pedrera is sold to an estate agent's but Roser Segimon continues to reside in her apartment.

1964
Roser Segimon dies and the apartment is emptied, which she had occupied for more than 50 years.

1966
An insurance company rents and renovates the main apartment in order to set up office.

1986
Caixa Catalunya acquires the house and, in 1990, transforms the main floor into an exhibition room.

Details on the main floor

From the ceiling to the flooring, Gaudí pays attention to detail to the artistic works that enrich the residence of the Milà family.

Ceilings. Like whirlpools, the undulations are a characteristic of the ceilings on the main floor.

Art in plaster

The ceilings and the mouldings, authentic craftsmanship in plaster, carry out an important role in the interior of the flat on the main floor. They are inspired by whirlpools and vegetable forms that, worked as reliefs and perforations, accentuate the feeling of movement. Under the direction of Gaudí, in these works the architect Jujol made the most of the ductility of plaster in order to include inscriptions such as *we are still free* or Mary's anagram.

Inscriptions on the ceiling

The "M" for Mary on a ceiling

Josep Maria Jujol
His personal calligraphy can be recognized in the decoration of some ceilings and columns.

The mouldings
Finishing off the doors and all of the inside arches of the apartment, the mouldings are carried out in cane, plaster and burlap.

The door on the main floor
Of large size and made from walnut, it is delicately carved in relief with curves and undulations.

The floors

Gaudí employs different types of flooring to differentiate the rooms in the house according to the function they carry out. For areas of greater transit, such as corridors and vestibules, he applied slabs of Sénia stone; for the leisure areas, lounges and bedrooms, he used the warmth of parquet; and, for the service area such as the kitchen, the bathrooms and other rooms, he used different hydraulic tiles.

The lounge. The floors are laid with starred parquet, in which oak and beech are combined.

The tiles
When designing the tiles, Gaudí is inspired by marine life, such as snails and starfish.

Tile 14cm sideways

Seaweed
Its shapes are reproduced in relief.

The seasnail

The starfish

The corridors. They are paved, of ochred tones, with stone from Sénia, a village to the south of Tarragona.

The paving on Passeig de Gràcia
In the sixties and in homage to the architect, the City Council paves the Passeig de Gràcia with the flagstones designed by Antoni Gaudí.

Gaudí's tiles. Every three tiles comprise of a sea snail figure, a star and seaweed.

The games room. Employs the hydraulic tiles that, united, recreate delicate marine reliefs.

The rented apartments
Irregular rooms that search for functional use and light

Gaudí designs all the rented apartments, from the first to the fourth floor, to make the most of the light that comes from the exterior façades and from the rear façade. Although the flats have different structures and different rooms, the most striking spaces, lounges and bedrooms, look out on to the Passeig de Gràcia or Provença Street, and the service areas look out on to the luminous interior patios.

Functional organization

All of the flats share the same criteria of functional organization, which consists of seeking out natural light from the exterior façades in order to illuminate the lounges and bedrooms, while the interior patio's façades provide light to the service areas, kitchens and bathrooms. Nonetheless, the flats have different dimensions and irregular distributions given that, by being based on an open-plan design, partitions can be positioned in any area. To access the four floors of rented apartments, Gaudí created an innovative system where the lift is the main means of access and the stairs, the secondary.

15 RENTED APARTMENTS are distributed throughout the building: one next to the Mila's main flat, three on the first floor, four on the second and third, and three more on the fourth floor.

Patio

Patio
Its amplitude allows natural light to enter all the flats, including those on the lower floors.

Service staircase

The hall in the flats
Using the lift as main access, the tenants arrived directly up to the landing and door of their flats.

The service staircase
Gaudí devised three service staircases, one situated in the middle of the building and the other two in the rear part of the apartments.

Section

The profile of the building allows one to appreciate the arrangement of the different floors of the house and the vertical communication by means of one of the three service staircases.

La Pedrera today

Declared a World Heritage Site by UNESCO in 1984, La Pedrera now functions as headquarters to the Caixa Catalunya foundation and is open to the public as a cultural and exhibition centre. Despite the fact that the house is a historical and touristic monument, it continues conserving the essence of a residential building as some families still continue to reside in five of its flats.

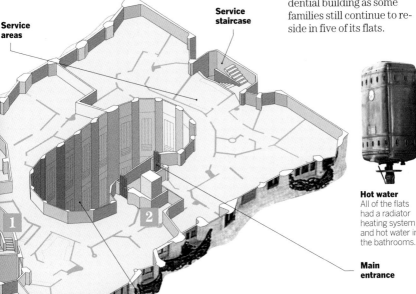

Service areas

Service staircase

1

2

Patio

Hot water

All of the flats had a radiator heating system and hot water in the bathrooms.

Main entrance

Lift

Of large dimensions, its cabin is made of wood and includes a rest bench, typical of the period.

Communication with the lift

Next to the front door, an intercom is connected to the porter's lodge, situated on the ground floor.

Renting permits

The Milàs asked the City Council for permission to let out the flats in 1910, but they couldn't do so until Gaudí signed the end of construction work in October of 1912. The architect and the Milàs also agreed that they would never sell one of the flats.

Luxury residences

Gaudí created spacious first class apartments, endowing them with many services and exquisite decorative finishes.

A space to enjoy

Gaudí designed all of the apartments in La Pedrera to be of large dimensions, from 290 to 600 metres square, to incorporate spacious leisure areas, such as the lounges on the façade sides, and service areas that were also ample, with roomy kitchens and three full-sized bathrooms. This solution guaranteed the comfort and smooth running of the flats.

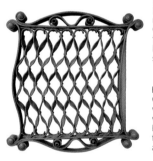

The lounges
The dining room and the living room of the apartments faced the exterior façades and had a balcony.

1912
THE FIRST TENANTS moved into the apartments in the month of December, two months after Gaudí signed the end of La Pedrera's construction work.

Look-out grille
Gaudí designs, with ribbons of wrought iron, the look-out grilles for the doors of all the flats.

The reception room. The entrance point to the flats is as spacious as the other service areas.

Toilets. All the flats have three full-sized bathrooms and a small ancillary one.

Bedroom. With wooden floors, it looks out on to the exterior façade, enjoying good illumination.

Objects designed by Gaudí
Although Gaudí didn't create much furniture for La Pedrera, the house now exhibits some objects that the architect designed for other buildings.

Mirror
Designed for Casa Calvet.

Chair
Designed for Casa Batlló.

Corridors. Luminous, they skirt the central patios and organize transit inside the apartments.

Window. It is finished off with mouldings.

Maximum comfort
The flats enjoyed all the comforts of the period: electric lighting, heating and hot water in the bathrooms. Moreover, all the tenants had the right to use a laundry room in the attic and a garage and lumber room in the basement. Gaudí had also planned that the balconies include an automatic watering system for the plants.

FAMOUS TENANTS
Over the years La Pedrera has housed the ex Minister of the Congo, Moise Tshombe, singers like Andy Russell and Salomé, and the son of writer André Maurois.

The doors
Gaudí wanted to make them from oak, but due to their high cost only two were made.

DATA
DISTRIBUTION OF THE APARTMENTS

The flats change their distribution from the first to the fourth floor, all being different thanks to the structure of the open-plan design devised by Gaudí.

1° This floor is divided into three independent flats.

2° Four flats make up the second floor.

3° The third floor houses four different apartments.

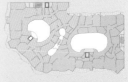

4° Three apartments occupy the last floor of flats.

FURNITURE AND ACCESSORIES

Gaudí's stamp is apparent on the decorative accessories, the artisanal work on different materials and the furniture he designed for the Milà family home.

The handles follow curved lines

THE BRASS WORK

1

Handles
Attached to the doors, they are sculptural objects whose shapes perfectly adapt to the hand and facilitate manipulation.

THE FURNITURE

2

Bench cupboard
Located in the hall of the Milàs' house and totally designed in wood, it allows the storage of different objects by lifting the bench's lid.

3

Chest
Of oak, carved on four sides and with a lock and brass key, this piece of furniture was used to divide two areas.

THE DECORATION

5

Applied arts
This piece, done by Josep Llimona in golden wood and ivory stuccowork, was designed for the Milà family's residence.

6

Clock
The clock's style, designed in wood, brass and gold leaf, fitted in perfectly with the undulating ceilings of the main floor of La Pedrera.

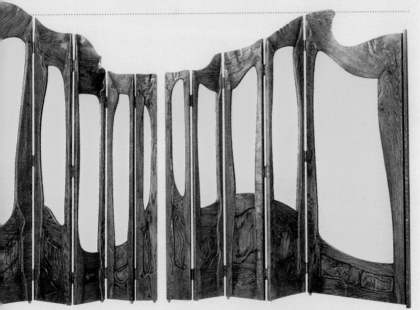

6

4

Folding screen
One of the most expressive pieces of furniture, it is done in oak and carved with organic forms, and is completed with rose coloured stained glass that lightens its dimensions: four metres wide by almost two metres high.

Detail
The doors are also carved with organic motifs in line with the other furniture.

07

01. Ironing room. The service areas had enough space to carry out the habitual different domestic tasks of the period. **02. Kitchen.** The ample space in the kitchen is organized into two sections, one for cooking and the other where the servants would eat. **03. Games room.** The flats had a room expressly for the leisure of the children and adults. **04 to 06. Mouldings.** Done in plaster, mouldings of organic shapes with signs and letters decorate all the doorframes and windows. **07. Hall.** The main entrances of the rented flats are found in large windowed halls, which can only be reached by lift.

06

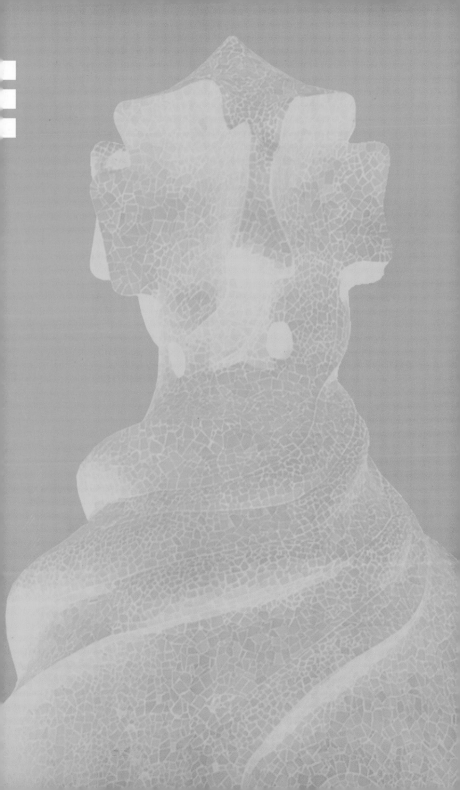

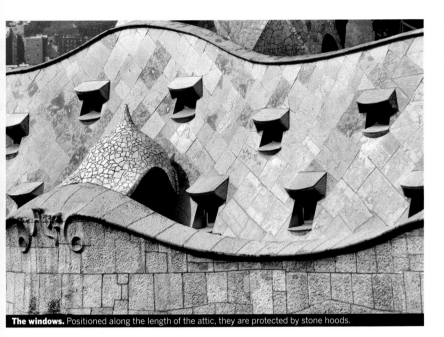

The windows. Positioned along the length of the attic, they are protected by stone hoods.

THE ATTIC

A functional skeleton

Gaudí crowns La Pedrera with a unique space where aesthetics and functional use combine.

Gaudí tackles the last floor, the attic, as the great coronation of La Pedrera, as much from the plastic point of view as the functional, in a way that the floor is endowed with its own architectonic system and some clearly marked original forms. It is a structure independent from the other floors of flats, a structure over another structure and a space with a different task and personality. Gaudí devised the attic as a protection chamber for the building in the face of extreme temperatures, whether in summer or winter, a thermal regulator inspired in the model of the Catalan attic, common in farms and in ancestral homes. However, instead of building this insulating chamber with walls and beams in the traditional manner, the architect planned 270 brick arches, of different heights and widths, but all of them parabolic, in other words, similar to an open curve and symmetrical in respect to an axis. Moreover, these arches, on which the terrace roof rests, create an undulating sequence charged with movement within the attic. Therefore, this area emerges as open-plan and continuous, without walls or columns to inhibit fluidity, whose arches evoke an organic space resembling the inside of a large animal.

Sentry walk
Allows the circumnavigation of the attic.

The attic

An independent architectonic structure

Gaudí topped the building with an attic, which was built some metres within the façade line and surrounded by a sentry walk. This final floor notably differs from the rest of the house and its exterior is covered with fragments of white stone, which contrast with the roughness and undulations of the façades, and it is peppered with small windows, which differ from the large windows on the lower floors.

The attic
Situated over the last floor of apartments, the attic has a different structure to the rest of the property in which Gaudí marks out the function and special character of this space.

The stone
The attic is covered over with regular pieces of stone from Ulldecona, a village in the south of Tarragona.

The windows
The upper windows of the attic are smaller than the lower ones, which measure 50 by 50 centimetres.

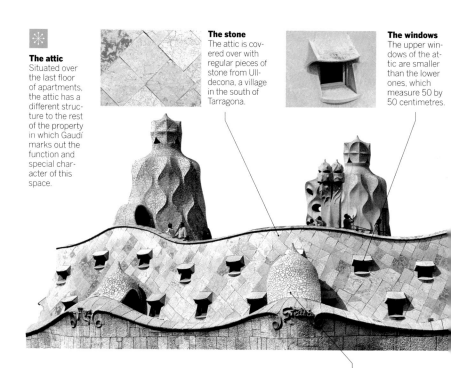

The thermal regulator
Gaudí designed the attic as an independent structure so it would act as an insulation chamber and provide protection for the building against extreme temperatures. This structure was completed with a ventilation system comprising of two types of windows, the small ones on the higher part of the walls and the big ones in the lower part, which had to be opened in the summer to create a current of air and be closed in winter to maintain the microclimate generated by the sun and the bricks. Due to its function as thermal regulator, the attic was also the area intended for installing laundry rooms and washing lines, which all tenants had at their disposition.

The cupolas
Of parabolic profile, four small cupolas cover part of the sentry walk.

Antoni
Gaudí

**Buildings must have a
double protection, just
like dignitaries wear a
hat and cloak"**

The attic and the Provença patio

Sentry walk over Provença. It goes around the perimeter of the house.

Stairwell

**160
WINDOWS**
of two sizes are
distributed
throughout the
attic's perimeter.

Starting point of the arches

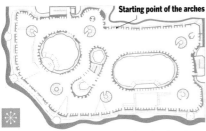

The plan view. Free from partitions, the plan view shows
the layout of the attic around the patios, the sentry walk
surrounding it and the starting point of the arches.

?

**WHAT IS
A SENTRY
WALK?**
It is a narrow
walkway
that, over the
walls of a
castle, is
used to con-
nect the tur-
rets and
keep guard.

Sentry walk rear. Of sinuous
curves, the stretches are of unequal
width and some have ramps.

The inside of the attic

*With a potent evocative capacity,
the interior forms a continuous and
fluid space of great formal complexity.*

An open floor

The attic's structure is totally different to that of the rest of the building, as it is designed as a continuous floor measuring 800 metres square, without columns or walls that interrupt circulation. Gaudí creates the attic from 270 arches of different height, width and layout that generate a constant spatial change and which appear to be inspired by the diaphragm of a huge animal or the inside of a cave.

Inside the attic
This open and spacious area was planned to house the community services of the entire house. With this function in mind, Gaudí designs a structure that is based on brick or catenary arches that support the walls and the ceiling.

The nodes
In the staircases that climb up to the terrace roof, various arches of differing heights are connected, creating new forms that enrich the attic space.

The *Espai Gaudí*

After the renovation, which was completed in the year 1996, the attic of La Pedrera has been home to the *Espai Gaudí*, which, as an exhibition area, offers a full vision of the life and work of Gaudí, his main innovations and their historical context. Amongst the elements exhibited in this space, stand out various models of buildings created by the architect.

The exhibition. It shows many models of Gaudí's works and the construction of La Pedrera.

The funicular. The model, developed by the *Espai* recreates the invention that Gaudí used in some of his works.

Model
Situated on the *Espai Gaudí*, the attic's structure can be discovered- its arches and windows, and the stairwell to the terrace.

Architect Francisco Barba Corsini
He planned the renovation of the attic, converting it into thirteen apartments for rent.

LOCATION

The apartments

In 1946 Roser Seimon sells La Pedrera to a real estate company. In 1953, in order to profit more from the investment, architect, Barba Corsini is entrusted with the project of converting the attic into rented penthouses. In this remodelation the bricks of the arches are rendered over and three apartments of modern aesthetic are created, in tune with European design of the period. All the residences have a lounge, bedrooms and, some, a mezzanine, including direct access to the terrace roof. However, this intervention altered the concept of the ventilation chamber that Gaudí had devised for the attic.

1954
WAS THE YEAR
when the penthouses designed by architect Barba Corsini were constructed.

13
PENTHOUSES
occupy the attic area of La Pedrera.

Barba Corsini's project
Included the furniture and the decoration.

Model of basement. In the *Espai Gaudí* is the model of the radial beam structure, in the shape of a bicycle wheel, which Gaudí built in the basement.

RESTORATION
THE ORIGINAL APPEARANCE IS RECUPERATED

The re-opening in 1996 of the attic, which recuperated Gaudí's concept, concludes the first restoration of La Pedrera. After knocking down the apartments, the arches were built again, the structure was refitted, the metal structure was strengthened and natural light planned by the architect was returned.

An organic structure

The parabolic arches in the attic designed by Gaudí create a structure that combines simplicity and resistence.

The construction

In spite of the arches being of different height and extension, the attic is a structure of great formal unity. Constructed on top of the last wrought iron structure, it was there that Gaudí designed the arches. This was done by marking the width of the arch on a high wall and fixing two nails to indicate where it started. Later a chain was hung between the nails until its lower point coincided with the height determined by Gaudí. Then the curve of the chain was drawn on the wall, and this was copied in wood, obtaining a wooden arch over which, once turned 180 degrees and put into place, the builders laid the bricks in order to construct the final arch. To strengthen their connection, the arches were united by means of a rib that joined them in longitudinal direction.

Series of arches
Each one of the arches was erected with courses of bricks that were placed on their sides and followed the curve marked out by Gaudí.

Arches constructed with bricks

Unevenness of the terrace

Stairwell

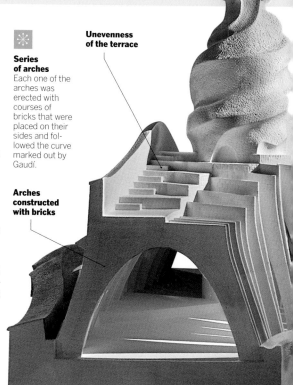

The rib. A longitudinal axis, formed by courses of bricks placed on their sides, joins all the arches.

Palm tree node. On one of the walls twelve arches are united, creating a brick palm tree.

Distribution of the arches. Laid out in series, the attic arches generate a fluid and continuous space.

The structure of a boat
The arch system in the attic, created by Gaudí, has been compared to the structure of an inverted boat.

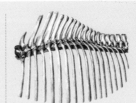

Organic inspiration
Other theories point out the similarity of the attic with the thorax of a voluminous animal, like a whale.

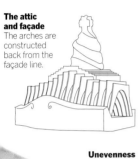

The attic and façade
The arches are constructed back from the façade line.

Unevenness of the terrace

In full construction. Situated at the height of the fifth floor, the construction of the attic was carried out with a simple system of wooden mouldings.

270
ARCHES
different catenary arches shape the structure of the attic, which supports the house's terrace roof.

Gaudí's arches

As in the attic of La Pedrera, a good part of Gaudí's works resort to the catenary arch system, which is used for example in the loft of Casa Batlló or the naves of Sagrada Familia. The architect was especially fond of these arches as structural elements. He named them balancing arches because their shape, like a chain hanging from its ends and seen upside down, allows the even distribution of the load and transforms the arch into a resistant structure in itself so that it doesn't require buttresses nor other support elements such as Romanesque and Gothic arches. Moreover, its brick construction is simple and inexpensive.

DATA
COINCIDENCES AND SIMILARITIES

With the complicity of the constructor Bayó, the architect Puig i Cadafalch secretly visited the construction work. Shortly after, he built the Codorníu wine cellars with arches similar to those in the attic.

01. Perimeter rib. The upper part of all the arches on this floor is joined by means of a course of bricks to provide them with greater resistance. **02. Staircases.** The six cylinders housing the stairs possess a series of hollows, designed by Gaudí to improve the ventilation. **03 and 04. Joins.** The joins of the arches seem to be inspired in organic structures. **05. Interior arches.** The series of catenary arches of different height and width create a continuous and fluid space. **06 and 07. The attic exterior.** The exterior part of the attic that looks out on to the main façades is covered over in stone and the part that looks out on to the rear façade and interior patios is rendered over and painted.

07

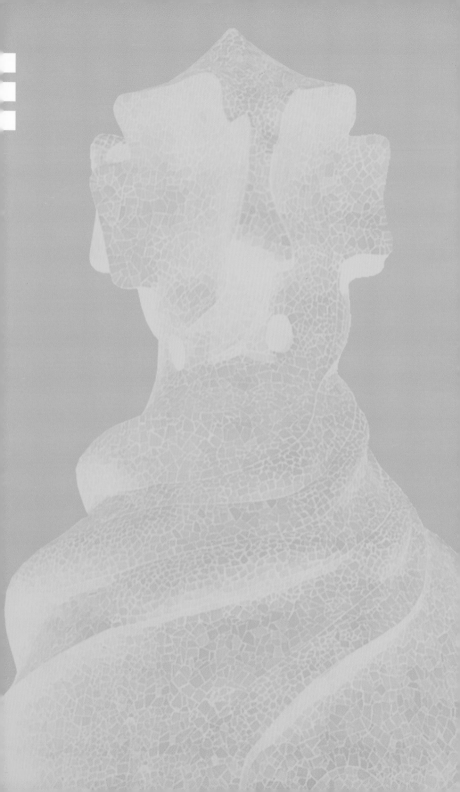

The forms. The undulating lines increase the evocative power of the terrace.

THE TERRACE

A universe of artistic forms

Gaudí transcends functionalism by transforming the terrace into a magical space charged with insinuations.

On the terrace of La Pedrera, Gaudí deploys all his creative and expressive ability, transforming this area, which at the start of the 20th century was hardly considered when planning a building, into a universe of shapes, silhouettes and original textures that transcend architecture and become an artistic work in their own right. From a formal point of view, the architect's first intention was that the terrace would top the building in harmony with the undulating rhythms that characterize the façade. Then, that the terrace, comprising of sections of varying volumes, would ascend and descend generating different levels connected by stairs that vary in number of steps, size and shape. This staggered structure adheres to the uneven heights of the attic arches, over which, precisely, rests the terrace. Moreover, Gaudí resolves the necessary functions of the terrace by grouping together and organizing the arrangement of elements on this floor: the stairwells, the chimneys and the ventilation towers. Transformed into sculptural works, these fantastical forms have been interpreted in different ways and through time related with different symbolic elements. Thus, the architect, combining art and architecture, creates a unique space that is extremely insinuative and evocative.

Stairwell

The terrace

A magical space with surprising shapes

Expressiveness and aesthetic freedom pervade the creation of the terrace, where the stairwells, chimneys and ventilation towers emerge as authentic sculptures. The three-dimensional forms of these elements break up and organize the routes of the steps, which connect the differing levels of the terrace that Gaudí managed to imbue with an intense and original artistic dimension.

A landscape of forms

The terrace is constructed over the attic following the different heights marked out by the arches which Gaudí built this space with. These variations result in small runs, raised at different levels and united by stairs of different widths; a structure whose mission is to avoid the terrace cracking, which is caused by expansion and contraction of material in hot and cold weather. Rising over this terrace of uneven height and spaces is an arrangement of surprising sculptural elements, of varying sizes and geometric forms, which correspond to three very different functions: access to the terrace, ventilation shafts and smoke vents.

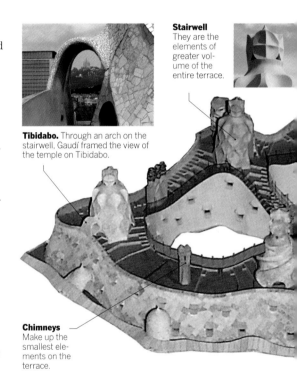

Tibidabo. Through an arch on the stairwell, Gaudí framed the view of the temple on Tibidabo.

Stairwell
They are the elements of greater volume of the entire terrace.

Chimneys
Make up the smallest elements on the terrace.

RESTORATION
FORMS AND COLOURS ARE RECUPERATED

The terrace is restored in 1995 to repair the structure and rescue the original shapes, textures and colours, but above all to recuperate all the elements actually designed by Gaudí. Therefore, some chimneys that were later added are eliminated during the renovations.

Elements on the terrace. Its figures rise and fall according to the undulations marked out by the attic.

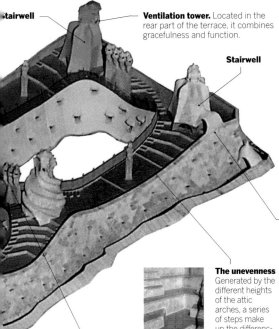

Stairwell

Ventilation tower. Located in the rear part of the terrace, it combines gracefulness and function.

Stairwell

The unevenness Generated by the different heights of the attic arches, a series of steps make up the differences in height of the terrace.

Group of chimneys

Sagrada Familia. The architect frames the view of the imposing temple by means of one of the arches.

 DATA
THE LOCATION OF THE ELEMENTS

While the two ventilation towers rise in the rear part of the terrace, the chimneys border the interior patios and the six stairwells are in line with the façades.

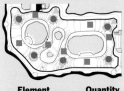

Element	Quantity
■ Chimneys	30
▲ Ventilations	2
● Stairwells	6

" The terminations of buildings with paltry elements, like crosses, weather vanes etc., are really caricatures, like a bald person with only one hair in the middle. **"**

Antoni Gaudí

38
DIFFERENT ELEMENTS were built by Gaudí on the terrace of the house, 30 chimneys in seven groups, two ventilation towers and six stairwells.

Stairwells

These surprising elements are one of Gaudí's maximum expressions as a creator of forms.

Geometry and dimensions
These curved forms, derived from ruled geometry, lighten the great volume of the stairwells.

Access to the terrace

Of larger size than the other elements on the terrace, each one of the six stairwells contains a water deposit in its upper section and connects with the attic by means of a winding staircase. Moreover, they have a series of hollows that help to renew the air in the attic. Gaudí designed four different models of conical form that, covered with *trencadís*, correspond to the four exits lined up with the exterior façades. Of the six models, two are quite similar and another two are repeated in ochre stuccowork by the stairwells that are situated near the rear façade.

Two variants
For the two most important stairwells, the most visible ones from the street, Gaudí created two models of twisting forms that turned in opposite direction.

Zenith view
Reveals the helicoidal lines with which these constructions are generated.

Trencadís
of white colour decorates the four stairwells that look out on to the Passeig de Gràcia and Provença Street.

6
STAIRWELLS
connect the attic floor with the terrace.

Other forms
Two of the stairwells are bell-like, also crowned with volumetric crosses, but have different finishes.

Materials
Gaudí covered four stairwells with a trencadís of marble and white ceramic work, and used ochre stuccowork on the other two.

7,80
METRES
is the height of the highest stairwell, located in the area corresponding to the chamfered corner façade.

LOCATION

The volumetric cross
Placed over the chamfered corner façade, Gaudí topped this stairwell with a cross whose four sides face the cardinal points.

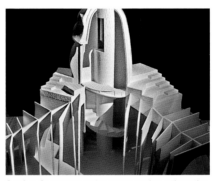

Section. Shows the winding staircase that coils up the inside of the terrace stairwells.

Inscription
On one of the stairwells the phrase *M.* (for Mary) 1910 *Rebled*, is engraved, which alludes to the building's first caretaker.

Ventilation hollows

The curl
Gaudí modelled the stairwells with helicoidal lines, like those generated when twisting a ductile material.

The meringue
The figures on the stairwells remind of decorations, like the meringue, which is used in baking.

Differing interpretations

The sculptural constructions of the stairwells constitute one of Gaudí's creations that has given rise to the largest number of theories and lectures. These surprising figures have been interpreted as a version of *Wonderland*, a series of dancing giants, a procession of gentlemen, cake decorations, giant Catalan Easter eggs and also, the different crags on the mountain of Montserrat.

Geometric. The sinuous lines form concave and convex areas.

Ventilation towers

The two figures of the ventilation towers play with subtle undulations and move closer to the shapes of abstract sculpture.

Two special towers

In line with the rear façade that looks out on to the block courtyard, two towers join the ventilation shafts coming from the basement and, in this way, help to simplify and organize the elements that appear on the terrace. Constructed as brick vaults and plastered with mortar of yellowish tones, the towers rise with slim organic forms following two models: one of hexagonal ground plan similar to a covered goblet, and another that appears to be geometrically comprised of various Mobius strips perforated by circular holes.

5.40 metres

Organic shape
The original volumes of the ventilation towers seem to correspond to vegetable or anthropomorphic forms.

Zenith view
Divided into six equal parts, it shows the geometric structure designed by Antoni Gaudí.

2
VENTILATION TOWERS
rise on the terrace to group together the different ventilation shafts coming from the basement.

MODELS
All the elements on the terrace are first made into plaster models and, later, are copied into their real size.

In construction. The constructor of La Pedrera, Josep Bayó, who is second on the right, poses on the terrace during building work.

The tower
Front and lateral view of the tower that is similar to the shape of a covered goblet, with a big, vertical, oval opening.

Salvador Dalí
Fascinated by the shape of the chimneys, the Surrealist did a photographic report on the terrace in 1951.

5,60 metres

View of the terrace. The tower blends into the geometry of the terrace.

The goblet. Emerging behind the stairwell is the goblet ventilation tower.

The power of evocation

Due to their imaginative design, the ventilation towers haven't escaped diverse metaphorical interpretations either. Some consider them as an anticipation of the Surrealist movement for the use of smooth forms that evoke oneiric images. Other theories maintain that one of the two towers is a mask or monstrous face with various eyes, maybe inspired by the Cubist figures of Picasso, and the other, a covered goblet with a hat, or the female sexual organ, symbol of desire.

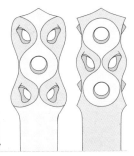

Drawing in view. Its outlines and hollows back the theory that this tower evokes a mask.

The chimneys

Gaudí transforms traditional chimneys into suggestive and evocative sculptural structures.

The chimneys. They are constructed with pieces of brick forming a vault and later rendered over with mortar.

Stylised figures

The smallest elements on the terrace are the chimneys, which are organized into seven groups, coming to a total of 30 vents. They rise up surrounding the patios eliminating the fumes from the kitchens and flats and the heating boilers in the basement. Although all answer to the same concept, a trunk that revolves around itself topped with a type of cupola, some are individual and others comprise of groups of two, five, six or eight. The chimneys have an ochre colour finish, but standing out is a group covered with fragments of bottles of cava.

Symbolism. Some chimneys have crosses, letters x and other signs connected to Gaudí.

The groups
Some of the chimneys branch out, stemming from a common trunk, in groups of two, five, six or seven arms.

Soldiers
The sculptor Subirachs was inspired by these chimneys when creating the soldiers on the Passion façade of the temple of the Sagrada Familia.

LOCATION

Hypotheses and theories
From the start, the stylised figure of the chimneys summon up different ideas, such as groups of patrolling desert warriors with helmets and their faces hidden, women's faces, groups of owls, mushrooms, geographical forms and even a chorus of musicians and singers which rise up accompanying the rest of the other elements.

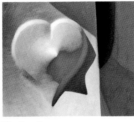

The heart
On one of the chimneys Gaudí positioned a heart facing Reus, his city of birth, in order to symbolize his love for his roots.

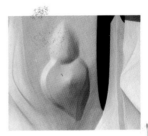

The heart and the tear. On the other side of this chimney, a heart and a tear look out towards the Sagrada Familia; believed to express Gaudí's sadness for not concluding this work.

Cava
According to a legend, the glass that decorates some chimneys comes from the bottles consumed at the house's inauguration party.

30 CHIMNEYS
rise up, in groups or individually from the terrace.

STAR WARS
It is believed that George Lucas, who visited La Pedrera before directing the saga *Star Wars*, was inspired by the chimneys to create the imperial soldiers and Darth Vader.

THE ELEMENTS ON THE TERRACE

The surprising sculptural figures designed by Gaudí transform the terrace into an artistic and mysterious space, and enhance the monument's evocative power.

7,80
METRES

The colour
Ochre tones abound on the terrace, except for the four stairwells covered in white *trencadís* work that look out on to the exterior façade and are seen from the street.

The stairwells
Crowned with crosses, they are constructed following four different models, two of them being very similar to each other.

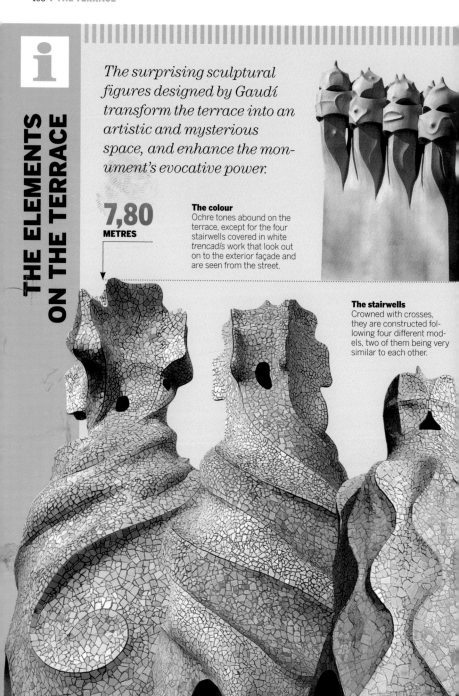

Chimneys
Of very similar shapes, Gaudí created the chimneys parting from a curling trunk and crowned with a cowl. However, one group stands out for the bottle glass it is covered with, which acts as impermeable protection as well as aesthetic detail.

6,80
METRES

Trencadís
Combines marble and ceramic work to achieve two contrasting white areas.

The ventilation towers
Gaudí projected two ventilation towers in two different formats, but both are of anthropomorphic inspiration.

5,60
METRES

5,40
METRES

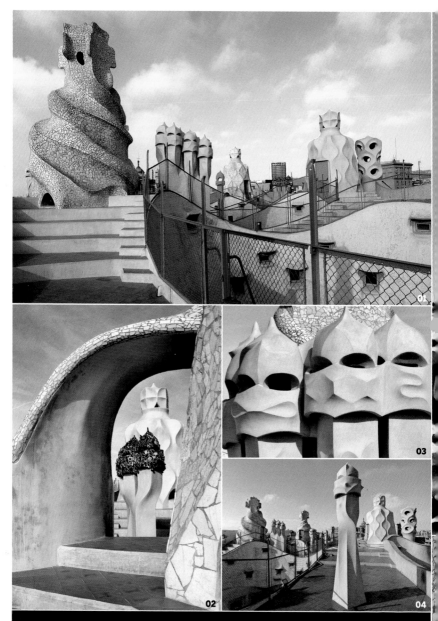

01, 02 and 04. Perspectives. Gaudí transformed the terrace of La Pedrera into a suggestive and evocative artistic landscape. **03. The chimneys.** These fantastic forms incite all types of interpretations: warriors, women, birds, and even a chorus of musicians. **05. The bottles of cava.** On one of the groups of chimneys the cowls are covered with fragments of bottles of cava. **06. The curl.** The stairwells are finished with *trencadís* and geometric figures are drawn on some of them. **07. Volumetric crosses.** Gaudí topped the stairwells with three or four-sided crosses. **08. Restoration.** On one of the tiles of the trencadís work on the stairwells is engraved the year in which the terrace was restored.

VISUAL GUIDE OF LA PEDRERA, CASA MILÀ

© PUBLISHED BY
2008, DOS DE ARTE EDICIONES, S.L.

TEXTS
MANAGING DIRECTORS:
CARLOS GIORDANO AND NICOLÁS PALMISANO.
REDACTION: ALBERTO RODRÍGUEZ AND LIONEL SOSA
(CHAPTERS 1 AND 3 TO 7).
XAVIER GONZÁLEZ TORÁN (CHAPTER 2).
TRANSLATIONS: CERYS R. JONES.
© CARLOS GIORDANO AND NICOLÁS PALMISANO

© PHOTOGRAPHS
ALL OF THE PHOTOGRAPHS ARE BY
CARLOS GIORDANO AND NICOLÁS PALMISANO
WITH THE FOLLOWING EXCEPTIONS:

• ARXIU CÀTEDRA GAUDÍ, pag. 004, 006, 027, 042, 043, 093, 104.
• ARXIU ESPAI GAUDÍ, CENTRE CULTURAL CAIXA CATALUNYA,
  pag. 012, 039 (ROSER SEGIMON AND PERE MILÀ).
• ARXIU HISTÒRIC DE LA CIUTAT DE BARCELONA – ARXIU
  FOTOGRÀFIC, pag. 010, 011 (UNKNOWN AUTHORS).
• ARXIU NACIONAL DE CATALUNYA, pag. 028 - PHOTOGRAPH #
  1 (PHOTOGRAPHER: BRANGULÍ).
• BODEGAS CODORNÍU, pag. 093.
• INSTITUT AMATLLER D'ART HISPÀNIC. ARXIU MAS, pag. 072.
• INSTITUT DE CULTURA DE BARCELONA, ARXIU HISTÒRIC DE
  LA CIUTAT, (CASTELUCHO) pag. 008.
• JUNTA CONSTRUCTORA DEL TEMPLE EXPIATORI DE LA
  SAGRADA FAMÍLIA, pag. 015 (GAUDÍ STUDY), PAG. 081 (PHO-
  TOGRAPH # 5, CASA MUSEU GAUDÍ).
• PEDRO UHART (WWW.GAUDIDESIGNER.COM),
  pag. 080, 081 (Nº 3, 4, 6).

ILLUSTRATIONS
• © CARLOS GIORDANO AND NICOLÁS PALMISANO, pag. 22,
  23, 24, 25, 34, 35, 37, 39, 41, 42, 43, 44, 45, 52, 53, 54, 55, 56,
  57, 60, 61, 62, 75, 76, 77, 79, 89, 91, 101, 102, 104, 105, 106, 107.
• GALERÍA H2O, pag. 091.
• ARXIU ESPAI GAUDÍ, CENTRE CULTURAL CAIXA CAT-
  ALUNYA, pag. 022 (SKETCHES BY PICAROL, PUBLISHED IN
  L'ESQUELLA DE LA TORRATXA, 1910 AND 1912), 045 (SKETCH
  BY F. BRUNET, PUBLISHED IN EL DILUVIO), 077 (SECTION).

THIRD EDITION, 2008

ISBN
978-84-934493-1-5

DEPÓSITO LEGAL
B-23352-2006

PRINTED IN SPAIN
I.G. MARMOL S.L.

The editor is at the disposition of owners of possible unidentified icongraphic sources.

WITH THE
COLLABORATION
OF THE

FUNDACIÓ CAIXA CATALUNYA

DOS De
aRTe
EDICIONES
www.dosdearte.com
info@dosdearte.com